Teambuilding

Daniel Roşu and Mihaela Diaconu (eds.)

Teambuilding

Instrument for Increasing Organizational Performance

PETER LANG

Berlin · Bruxelles · Chennai · Lausanne · New York · Oxford

Bibliographic Information published by the Deutsche Nationalbibliothek
The Deutsche Nationalbibliothek lists this publication in the Deutsche Nationalbibliografie; detailed bibliographic data is available in the internet at http://dnb.d-nb.de.

Library of Congress Cataloging-in-Publication Data
Names: Rosu, Daniel, 1964- editor. | Diaconu, Mihaela, 1966- editor.
Title: Teambuilding : instrument for increasing organizational performance / edited by Daniel Roşu and Mihaela Diaconu.
Description: New York : Peter Lang, [2025] | Includes bibliographical references.
Identifiers: LCCN 2025000541 (print) | LCCN 2025000542 (ebook) | ISBN 9783631915837 (paperback) | ISBN 9783631932162 (ebook) | ISBN 9783631932179 (epub)
Subjects: LCSH: Teams in the workplace.
Classification: LCC HD66 .T42155 2025 (print) | LCC HD66 (ebook) | DDC 658.4/022--dc23/eng/20250217
LC record available at https://lccn.loc.gov/2025000541
LC ebook record available at https://lccn.loc.gov/2025000542

ISBN 978-3-631-91583-7 (Print)
E-ISBN 978-3-631-93216-2 (E-PDF)
E-ISBN 978-3-631-93217-9 (E-PUB)
DOI 10.3726/b22618

Published by Peter Lang GmbH, Berlin (Germany)

info@peterlang.com

This publication has been peer reviewed.

www.peterlang.com

We dedicate this book to all those who believe in the power of collaboration, who want to transform workplaces into environments of excellence, and who seek to build authentic connections. May this book inspire you and give you the tools to guide your own journey in the art of teambuilding.

With gratitude for each contribution to building strong and connected teams
—Authors

Contents

Preface

From Homo ludens to Teambuilding

With a respectable age (the term appeared in the 1920–1930s when group dynamics and interpersonal relationships in the work environment began to be studied more and more), teambuilding—in the sense of organized activity with the stated purpose of improve collaboration and communication within a team—gained popularity in the 1970s and 1980s. Therefore, half a century of terminological remodeling, taxonomic nuances and interdisciplinary connections.

Because it goes beyond the boundaries of a simple "discipline," the teambuilding phenomenon is researched and approached mainly from the perspective of social and behavioral sciences: Organizational and industrial psychology studies human behavior in the organizational and work context, selecting as relevant motivation, communication, satisfaction at work, group dynamics, and team development. Social psychology explores how social interactions influence individual thoughts, feelings, and behavior to understand group dynamics and interpersonal relationships within teams. Organizational sociology examines the social structures and processes within organizations and how they influence employee behavior and performance, with a particular focus on the role of cultural influences within the organization.

We propose here two other areas of confluence. First, Cultural Anthropology is discipline concerned with the study of human culture, behavior, customs, values, and social interactions of different groups and communities. In teambuilding, cultural anthropology facilitates the understanding of the cultural context in which a team operates. This may involve understanding the norms, values, and modes of communication specific to the organizational culture or other cultural influences that may affect team dynamics. Then, the History of Mentalities, which probes collective mentalities, beliefs, perceptions, and representations, and how these have changed diachronically within a society. In the context of teambuilding, the history of mindsets provides a picture of how the collective ideas and values of a team/organization have developed over time and how they may affect collaboration and communication today. In other words, retrospective understanding of organizational culture can provide important clues to improving relationships and team performance today.

The work coordinated by Daniel Roşu and Mihaela Diaconu is based on an interdisciplinary project developed by teaching staff from the University of Pitesti: Design, testing, and validation of an innovative teambuilding product to increase organizational performance. Teambuilding, Tool for increasing organizational performance covers, in almost 200 pages, almost all the issues covered by the key concept. The material is structured in 10 information-dense chapters, happily combining the theoretical with the applied. The complementary points of view of those who contributed to the realization of this product are explained/justified on the one hand by the basic specialization of the authors, on the other hand, they are "brands" of the stylistic personality of each member of the team. From this perspective, the global text is also a result of some academic teambuilding activities.

The theoretical framework of the research is configured starting from the critical analysis of the specialized literature. The authors consider the following elements relevant to their approach: the effects of teambuilding activities on employees/organization; the factors that influence the design of teambuilding programs/products; teambuilding objectives and techniques; the application contexts of teambuilding; the purpose of these programs; the characteristics of teambuilding programs; types of teambuilding, etc.

Very useful for positioning in the context is the needs analysis carried out on a sample of about 100 organizations from the South-Muntenia Region. In addition, four focus groups were organized with important actors for these types of activities—human resources specialists, psychologists, top managers, and representatives of the executive of the companies involved. The analysis had two dimensions, one qualitative (it consisted in the identification of the determining factors, the characteristics, the effects of teambuilding programs, the links between teambuilding, and different individual or organizational variables), the other quantitative (it sought to measure the importance of the determining factors of teambuilding programs and correlating these factors with the effects, that is, identifying an ideal teambuilding program according to the type of company). Those characteristics that had the highest degree of occurrences were then selected, able to serve the development of conceptual models ("Antecedents and effects of teambuilding programs—an integrated approach: organizational and individual").

The other components that complete the set of teambuilding activities consider sets of sub-activities such as warm-up (with the meaning of preparatory actions) and knowledge, trust building, communication and collaboration, leadership and decision-making, problem solving in a simulated environment, feedback and reflection, relaxation, and socializing. For each thematic area, a specialized bibliography is provided, useful both to the informed reader and to the non-specialist in the field.

A few words about the title of prefect. Without pretending to solve the dilemma with which the book opens—How did sapiens survive Neanderthal Man?—I offer you the metaphorical solution: Homo ludens! Johan Huizinga's hypothesis derives from the idea that play is a fundamental activity of humanity, having a profound influence on culture, society and the way people interact with each other. This perspective is compatible with teambuilding in several ways: (1) Activities such as games, challenges, and group exercises can be seen as ways in which team members engage in a form of structured play. Participants use their creativity, competitive spirit, and collaborative ability to achieve set goals, thus reflecting the playful nature of human behavior. (2) Play is not only an entertainment activity, but also an important way for people to learn and develop. In the context of teambuilding, playful activities can provide experiential learning opportunities where participants can develop skills such as communication and collaboration in an interactive environment, leadership, and problem solving. (3) Play is often associated with building relationships and strengthening social bonds between participants. In teambuilding, fun activities can help create a relaxed and friendly environment where team members can develop confidence and strengthen group cohesion. (4) Last but not least, the game encourages non-conformist thinking, exploring new ideas, and innovative approaches. In teambuilding activities, participants are often asked to use their imaginations and come up with creative solutions to given problems, which can stimulate innovation and improve the team's ability to tackle challenges in novel ways.

To preserve the rules of the game, I invite you to join as dialogue partners of this book. After all, reading is a game of meaning when there is no consensus between sender and receiver.

Adrian Sămărescu, Ph.D., University Lecturer,
Vice-Rector Relations with Students, Graduates and
the Socio-Economic Environment, National University of Science
and Technology, Politehnica—Pitesti University Center

Foreword

Teambuilding actions are not the prerogative of a single discipline. They harmoniously combine elements of acting, literature, sports, educational sciences, and notions of psychology, as can be seen from the present material.

This book represents the quintessence of an interdisciplinary project, with the name "Design, testing and validation of an innovative teambuilding product to increase organizational performance," with the acronym: #team-INNOVATION_UPIT, project financed through the internal competition of inter-faculty projects, within the University of Pitesti, Romania. The project coagulates the experience and efforts of teaching staff from four distinct faculties—the Faculty of Sciences, Physical Education and Informatics, the Faculty of Educational Sciences, Social Sciences and Psychology, the Faculty of Economic Sciences and Law as well as the Faculty of Theology, Letters, History and Arts, all of these from the National University of Science and Technology POLITEHNICA Bucharest, Piteşti University Center.

Thus, at the academic level, teambuilding as a theme brought together the members of an academic community, succeeded in overcoming interdisciplinary barriers or positions or functions, by creating scientific links between participants, based on a better knowledge of all. At the end of the project, we want to believe that we have managed to create a high-performing team that is able to find, together with others, a key to success.

Teamwork is rather understudied in our schools, and the amazing development of technology brings to everyone an added loneliness, a rejection of collegiality. To compensate for this state of affairs, teambuilding generates a strategic and deliberate process of building cohesion and effectiveness within a team, using activities and exercises designed to develop trust, communication, collaboration, and interpersonal relationships among its members.

Introduction

Neanderthal and Homo sapiens! How did the second one emerge and the first one disappear? The answer to this question is complex and largely remains a matter of speculation, as there is no single universally accepted theory for the extinction of Neanderthal and the survival of Homo sapiens. However, there are several main theories that try to explain this phenomenon. Despite the evidence showing that these humanoid species interacted and even genetically intermingled, most researchers believe that sapiens may have had a superior ability to collaborate and innovate, aspects that could have provided an advantage competitive with Neanderthal. In his formidable evolution, modern humans have valued collaboration, far above interpersonal relations, teaming up with the horse, the elephant, the camel, or the dog, using with great success the qualities of these animals which they wisely perceived they did not possess.

The ability to collaborate has been one of the essential pillars that have contributed to the progress and development of human societies throughout history. Collaboration has had a significant impact in many areas and has been fundamental to the progress of society by generating innovation and technological development, division of labor and specialization, solving complex problems, scientific and medical progress, as well as the development of culture and the arts.

In order to make people collaborate better, society has made all kinds of interventions on several levels: education, the formation of support institutions, lifelong learning, or assisting organizations. Despite the emergence of false ideas about work, most people have realized that continuous and conscious involvement in the field of work is the most beneficial factor for man's passage through life, giving him purpose, direction, and satisfaction. Thus, in the contemporary period, the level of work has acquired increasing importance and responsibility, continuously adding more and more complicated forms of interaction with the employee. In the search for greater efficiency of economic processes, employee animation has become a viable solution within any type of enterprise or organization, large or small. Animating people in the field of work is today defined as an action specific to high-performance management, aimed at increasing the results and work efficiency of the members of the organization and contributing to the creation of an organizational culture conducive to obtaining high results.

The contemporary concept of teambuilding represents that type of activity that directly aims to improve the performance of an organization, by developing problem-solving skills, decision-making, conflict prevention and management, etc., within a work group. At the same time, it helps to abolish barriers and individual psychological stereotypes, increase confidence in one's own strength, increase tone, physical and mental condition, increase solidarity and responsibility. Teambuilding can support the construction of an organizational culture based on a high internal structure, with formal and informal relationships between individuals, with a high awareness of goals, and with activities designed to be carried out with high efficiency.

Teambuilding is, therefore, a process by which members of a team work together to develop closer relationships, to improve collaboration, communication, and mutual trust, as well as to develop individual and team skills. These activities aim to strengthen team spirit and create a more efficient and productive work environment.

Teambuilding projects often involve groups of people collaborating under stressful conditions. The themes proposed in teambuilding projects are expected to provide innovative solutions to emerging problems, to anticipate and respond to risks over which people have little control, and to delicately find the middle ground between the often-conflicting demands of the different groups of interested parties.

Chapter 1 attempts to create a solid framework for understanding and approaching the concept of teamwork. It includes several relevant topics to prepare the reader for further exploration of topics related to building and strengthening an effective team. This chapter provides an engaging and informative introduction to the world of teamwork, preparing the reader to explore in depth the specific teambuilding topics and strategies presented in the rest of the book. The chapter makes a cursory passage through the history of the emergence of the concept, up to its current evolution, including determining factors that can influence both the preparation and the implementation of the programs, the characteristics of the programs, the taxonomy of teambuilding, as well as the logical sequence of the types of activities.

Chapter 2 also has a theoretical basis by reviewing the specialized literature regarding the impact of teambuilding on organizational performance. The chapter starts by treating the problem of teambuilding and organizational performance as one of the innovative solutions to the emerging problems against the background of the anchoring of national economies in the world economy. Within the chapter, recourse is made to multiple dimensions, namely objectives, skills, and development programs.

Chapter 3 refers to the results of a needs analysis carried out by questioning the answers of about 100 organizations in the South-Muntenia Region, as well as four focus groups with important actors of this type of activity (with human resources specialists, psychologists, employees from executive and top managers). Following the quantitative and qualitative interpretation of the results, through the contribution of team members with expertise in different fields—economics, psychology, sports, acting-literature, the chapter offers a teambuilding product consisting of a concept (model), operationalization tools, methods, support materials (toolkit), strategies, and procedures, as well as a teambuilding guide.

Chapter 4 is devoted to warm-up and familiarization activities. Familiarity games help participants feel comfortable in each other's presence, and physical or mental warm-up exercises prepare participants for the main activities. The activities are organized for the purpose of getting to know the team partners better or "forced socialization." Such activities are welcome after fresh personnel changes, at the start of the company, or in the case of promoting a project that involves collaboration between different companies or branches. On the other hand, it is found more and more often that it is not enough that people work together for them to "get to know" each other, which implies the organization of an introduction in the atmosphere of a good mood. Introductory activities thus have the role of relaxing the atmosphere within the team. At the same time, they are used for the purpose of physical and mental preparation of the group to carry out some demanding activities. In many situations, these activities also create the muscle tone necessary to avoid accidents, as it is known that a warmed body responds better to the muscular effort, twists, stretches, and physical pressures required by the following activities. They are also used to overcome the artificial limits imposed by the work environment. The means used in this sense can be shouting, parodying situations, miming, ovations, etc.

Trust-building activities are presented in Chapter 5. The games and exercises in this link emphasize the development of trust and cooperation between team members, so they will encourage participants to associate and interact. Suitable means in this sense are movement games that can favor random "touches" between players.

In Chapter 6, communication and collaboration activities are presented. The games or exercises here call for effective communication and collaboration between team members. It is known that certain team tasks cannot be solved without team members collaborating through verbal and non-verbal communication. Each member must be consulted and considered either due to some competences in which he is an "expert," or due to some information that only he possesses through previous preparation of the activity.

Chapter 7 is dedicated to leadership and decision-making activities; the typical exercises described in this chapter provide opportunities for team leaders to stand out and develop their leadership skills. The chapter explains how these activities can involve choosing a leader, planning, and implementing a strategy for a specific task.

Chapter 8 is about problem-solving activities. The exercises require the team to identify and solve problems in a simulated environment. These activities may involve solving a complex scenario, making critical decisions, or managing limited resources. The chapter refers to activities to stimulate creativity and imagination with the aim of developing logical and creative thinking. These attributes are not aimed at the person and the group that can issue more and better ideas in solving some situations through collaboration. These ideas can also help confirm the competence of some members, destroy some preconceived ideas, build morale, and develop the spirit of camaraderie.

Chapter 9 is devoted to feedback and reflection activities. In this chapter, the role of deciphering the experience will be explained through discussions provoked by the organizers with the participation of the whole group, with positive sincerity and the identification of elements of vision. In feedback sessions, team members share observations and impressions about the team's performance. The chapter refers to discussions of what went well, what could be improved, and how lessons learned can be applied in the regular work environment.

Chapter 10 describes leisure and social activities. Although these activities are optional, they have a high frequency of use. The chapter shows that whenever space and time permit, relaxing activities or even parties can be organized to allow the team members to socialize and relax. This chapter insists on the fact that the use of human resources with a sense of humor and even the hiring of specialized teams can be of great importance.

CHAPTER 1

Teambuilding Theory

Daniel Roşu

Summary: The chapter constitutes an overview of teambuilding, summing up the presentation of the main concepts related to the subject. It begins by defining the term teambuilding, describes the historical connotations related to its emergence, and its connection with the development of the great economies of the globe. Gradually, the chapter demonstrates the significant impact of this type of activity on organizational performance and culture. Thus, it is shown that by promoting collaboration, effective communication, and the development of individual and team skills, teambuilding can positively influence both employees and the organization as a whole. In order to organize teambuilding activities, it is necessary to take into account several determining factors that can influence both the preparation and the running of the programs: the structure of the beneficiary team, the individual characteristics of the participants, the environment, and the competences demonstrated by the organizing and monitoring team. The chapter includes a taxonomy of teambuilding from the perspective of three basic criteria: the deployment environment (external and internal), the scope of deployment through classic and adventure activities, and according to the criterion of the sequence of implementation of the forms of activity. Finally, the chapter presents a sequence of applications of different types of teambuilding activities, as a preamble to the contents of Chapters 4–10.

Keywords: Objectives, history, evolution, typology, indoor, outdoor activities, adventure

Teambuilding activities involve direct interaction between participants, including outdoor activities, team games, and other exercises that involve close physical contact. The Covid-19 pandemic had a significant impact on all spheres of social and economic life, and also on teambuilding. The socio-economic response to adapt to this unprecedented situation for contemporaneity consisted of restrictions imposed to limit the spread of the virus. This has, in many cases, meant the dismantling of work teams and the widespread promotion of working from home in online conditions. Thus, the danger of de-individuation appeared, with strong psychological consequences of loss of identity, anonymity, frustration, and aggression.

After the pandemic, measures were imposed to restore social groups that stimulated individual activity, contributed to the development of the individual's ego and personality. As the general state of health improved, public policies everywhere suggested the implementation of measures to increase social cohesion in the workplace and restore the synergies of work groups, for a faster economic recovery.

In this context, teambuilding represented a safe way to readjust the organizational culture, based on active involvement and the readjustment of the original channels of human communication, the selection and promotion of leadership, in any social sphere.

The objectives of the teambuilding technique can vary, but the commonly used ones include:

- Increasing team cohesion.
- Teambuilding helps develop bonds between team members and creates a sense of unity and loyalty to common goals.
- Improving communication: Teambuilding activities can help improve communication skills among team members, which reduces misunderstandings and conflicts.
- Development of mutual trust: Team members get to know their colleagues better, which contributes to the development of mutual trust and respect.
- Encouraging collaboration: Teambuilding promotes teamwork and cooperation to achieve common goals.
- Improving individual and team skills: Participants can develop skills such as problem solving, decision making, leadership, and creative thinking.
- Creating a pleasant work environment: Teambuilding activities can help reduce stress, increase morale, and improve employee satisfaction.

Teambuilding can consist of a variety of activities, including games, confidence exercises, outdoor challenges, workshops, recreational activities, or even coaching and personal development sessions. These activities are designed to be fun and interactive, but also to provide practical learning that team members can apply in the professional context.

It is important that the teambuilding technique is customized according to the specific needs and goals of the team and the organization. Teambuilding can be used in various contexts, including business, non-governmental organizations, educational institutions, and many other organizations, to promote collaboration and effectiveness in groups of people working together.

1.1. The history of the emergence of teambuilding

The strong economies of the world, established after the middle of the twentieth century, such as the American and Japanese ones, demonstrated the effectiveness of teamwork through a series of experiments specific to collective activities, which generated particularly high economic results. The management of these economies has demonstrated unequivocally that it is not enough for people to work together, but it is necessary for them to collaborate, to subordinate their personal interest to the collective one, so that economic indicators, labor productivity, and, finally, the well-being of working people to improve continuously. In this context, the organizations discovered a new, interesting type of activity, carried out outside the concrete economic process, which aimed at building the team and forming the team spirit.

A brief history of the emergence of the teambuilding technique can be described in the distinct stages presented in the following:

- 1900–1930s—During this period, Frederick Winslow Taylor (1911) introduced the concept of "scientific management," which emphasized operational efficiency and the efficient organization of work within organizations. However, the concept of team development was still in its infancy during this period, and some of its ideas were later criticized for their excessive emphasis on productivity and efficiency, often ignoring the human and motivational aspects of work.
- 1940–1950s—After World War II, interest in applied psychology within organizations increased. Researchers such as Kurt Lewin and Abraham Maslow (1954) began to study employee behavior and motivation in the organizational context. Social field theory, the three-stage change model, group dynamics, and participative leadership approaches, and the theory of the hierarchy of human needs begin to significantly shape modern organizational theories.
- 1960–1970s—During this period, the first structured team development activities began to appear. In particular, Douglas McGregor's (1960) research on management styles (theory X and theory Y) influenced how managers began to perceive their approach to employees and their team. His theory emphasizes the differences in approach and behavior

of managers according to their fundamental beliefs about human nature and how this affects organizational management, inspiring management strategies and practices.

- 1980–1990s—This period marked a significant increase in the popularity of the teambuilding technique in the business environment. Various companies have sprung up specializing in facilitating team development activities. Various specific techniques and approaches have also been developed, such as role plays, simulations, and trust exercises.
- 2000s to present—With the advancement of technology and globalization, the teambuilding technique has continued to evolve. New ways to facilitate team development have emerged, including using online platforms and virtual communication technology.

Today, the teambuilding technique is widely used in organizations from various fields and industries (Cojanu et al., 2023). Companies recognize the importance of fostering collaboration, effective communication, and developing team skills to improve performance and productivity. Teambuilding is not just limited to recreational activities, but can also include training sessions, personal development workshops, and other methods designed to improve team cohesion and performance.

Teambuilding was imposed late in Romania, as a result of decades of stagnation in the development of organizational culture during the communist era. In the last decades, however, against the backdrop of the anchoring of the national economy in the global economy, of the emergence of multinational organizations, teambuilding is becoming more and more valued by the organizational management of many enterprises in our country.

1.2. Why teambuilding?

Viewed from outside the organization, teambuilding activities seem strange to say the least! Many people ask themselves, "Don't we waste enough time at work? Can't stand bosses, colleagues, or subordinates enough? Do I have to meet them in my free time too?" These are pertinent questions that require a satisfactory answer, and only a deep analysis can formulate acceptable answers. The purpose of these programs can be summarized in achieving one or more aspects mentioned in the following subsections:

- Obtaining a sense of individual mental comfort, performing unusual activities with colleagues.
- Gaining or regaining confidence in one's own strength to accomplish difficult tasks, by overcoming new situations.
- Gaining trust in co-workers through the help provided by them in specific teambuilding situations.
- Stimulating the talent, abilities, and creativity of the group members to achieve the objectives proposed in these activities.
- Discovering the strengths of team members, revealed as a result of responding to challenges of a different nature than those at work.

These goals are much higher than the minimal ones of obtaining a harmonious working environment, which is easy to achieve by creating a "group of friends" at the workplace, which, however, cannot be as effective as a well-strengthened team.

1.3. The impact of teambuilding on performance and organizational culture

Teambuilding is organized, in fact, because it has a significant impact on organizational performance and culture. By promoting collaboration, effective communication, and the development of individual and team skills, teambuilding can positively influence both employees and the organization as a whole, acting on several socio-psychological levels (Voicu, 2013). In the following, we will explain how to define the values that teambuilding aims at:

1.3.1. Increasing team cohesion and trust

Better cohesion: Through teambuilding activities, employees learn to communicate more effectively and better understand the working styles of their colleagues (Stefanica & Roşu, 2018). This leads to the reduction of misunderstandings and conflicts.

Building trust: A well-connected team that knows each other well will trust the skills and intentions of other team members.

1.3.2. Enhancing team spirit and sense of belonging

Encouraging cooperation: Through teambuilding activities, employees learn to work together towards a common goal, developing a sense of camaraderie and mutual support.

Cultivating Loyalty: When employees feel part of a united team, they will be more willing to actively engage in projects and remain loyal to the organization.

Stimulating creativity and innovation

Exploring unconventional solutions: Teambuilding activities can include challenges that require creative thinking and innovative approaches to solving problems or achieving goals.

Providing new insights: Close interaction between team members can bring to the surface new ideas and approaches that they might not have discovered individually.

Improving employee morale and satisfaction

Stress reduction: Participating in fun and constructive activities outside of the regular work environment can reduce employees' stress levels.

Emotional support: Teambuilding can create an environment where employees feel closer to each other and are more willing to offer support and encouragement to each other.

1.3.3. Developing skills and competencies

Enhancing teamwork skills: Teambuilding can provide a platform for developing collaborative, problem-solving, and decision-making skills in a group environment.

Identifying and capitalizing on individual talents: Teambuilding activities can bring out talents and skills that teammates might not normally notice.

1.3.4. Cultivating positive organizational culture

Promoting organizational values: Teambuilding can be used to emphasize the organization's values and goals, ensuring that all team members share them. In Figure 1.1, scenarios of voluntary activities in the mountain environment are presented.

Figure 1.1. Positive culture.

Encouraging commitment to the organization: A team that actively participates in teambuilding activities tends to be more engaged and contribute to the success of the organization (Voicu, 2013).

As a result of its attributes, teambuilding aims to achieve the most significant impact on organizational performance and culture, contributing to the development of a positive and productive work environment (Roşu et al., 2022). Of great importance, however, is the choice of teambuilding activities that suit the specific needs and values of the organization in order to achieve the best results.

1.4. The determining factors of teambuilding organization

In order to organize teambuilding activities, it is necessary to take into account several determining factors that can influence both the preparation and the running of the programs, as follows:

1.4.1. Structure of the beneficiary team

If the targeted team is numerous, it becomes difficult to hold group discussions in which all participants are involved. On the opposite pole, if the team includes only a few members, the activity itself may have contractions of physical, verbal, or psychological expression. In a small team, the heterogeneity of the team can be low and can influence the success of any activity due to self-censorship. Thus, the inclusion of members with a higher status (hierarchical superiors) in the targeted teams can inhibit discussions and even free expression within physical activities. Not unimportant is the fact that in the case of generating group discussions, there may be moments of silence or blockages in communication.

1.4.2. The individual characteristics of the participants

Personality differences within the team can ensure, when well-managed, the overall success of teambuilding programs. Sometimes, however, some participants do not stop talking, while others turn out to be very silent, in which case the instructor will have to facilitate equalizing the chances of all participants in decision-making and active involvement. On the other hand, on the level of physical training, heterogeneity can be a brake in the running of the programs, the organizers being in the dilemma of establishing the difficulties of the exercises. In these cases, either some will not get involved because the tasks are too difficult, or others will get bored because the tasks are too easy. The complexity of the challenges can brilliantly save these situations by creating mandatory positions with variable difficulties, within which each member can find their usefulness.

1.4.3. The deployment environment

The venue, the accommodation or meal conditions, the weather, the means used by the organizers, the atmosphere, all can influence the success of a predetermined teambuilding program. In this sense, it is first of all recommended to correctly inform the participants about the conditions offered, which implies a serious documentation of the organizers and even a visit to the location and the establishment of clear rules with the host (mealtimes, blackout times, the possibility of monopolization spaces without disturbing other tourists, etc. It is also necessary to prepare alternative programs of outdoor and indoor activities, the flexibility and adaptability of the organizers become crucial in some cases. For example, when the weather is very good, the participants might prefer some outdoor activities, even if the program was prepared to take place indoors, and vice versa, when the weather turns bad, the activities must be moved indoors and not carried out outside just for the sake of the prepared program.

1.4.4. The competences demonstrated by the organization and the monitoring team

The skills required for an organizing and monitoring team in teambuilding events may vary depending on the specific nature of the activities planned and the objectives of the event. However, in general, the following skills can be considered important:

- Knowledge of teambuilding: The team should have a solid knowledge of the fundamental principles and theories of teambuilding. This knowledge will help them plan and implement relevant and effective activities.
- Facilitation skills: Team members must have strong group facilitation and animating skills. This involves the ability to communicate effectively, manage groups, motivate participants, and create an open and cooperative environment.
- Creativity: The team should be able to generate ideas and create innovative and engaging activities. The ability to find creative solutions and adapt activities according to the needs and characteristics of the group is essential for the success of a teambuilding event.
- Communication skills: Team members must be able to communicate effectively with clients, participants, and among themselves. This includes active listening skills, clarity of expression, and adaptability in communication to meet the needs and expectations of different stakeholders.
- Time and resource management: The team must be able to effectively manage time, budget, and available resources to ensure the smooth running of the event. This involves planning, prioritizing, and quick problem-solving skills.
- Understanding of organizational needs: The team should have a clear understanding of organizational goals and the context in which the teambuilding event takes place. This will allow them to create relevant activities and incorporate elements that support the organization's values and culture.
- Evaluation and monitoring skills: The team should be able to evaluate the impact and effectiveness of teambuilding activities. This involves monitoring, evaluating, and gathering feedback skills to measure the success of the event and make necessary adjustments.

These skills should be supported by practical experience in organizing and monitoring teambuilding events. It is important that team members have solid experience in the field and can provide concrete examples and relevant case studies.

1.5. Characteristics of teambuilding programs

Teambuilding is neither strictly subordinated to didactic or sports activities, nor to employee training courses, nor to classic networking sessions, although it borrows from all of them some means and methods of learning and evaluation. For an easier understanding of the concept, in the following, we will resort to a presentation of the defining particularities of these activities.

1.5.1. Teambuilding promotes cooperation and not competition

In everyday life, many challenges are competitive, where the "many" lose and the "few" wins. Thus, we are suffocated by TV sports competitions, by those in stadiums and sports arenas, by cultural contests, by contests for occupying certain positions and positions, or by luck contests. Those who lose usually become unhappy, sometimes they lose confidence in their own strength, and most of the time they disassociate themselves from the winners (Roşu et al., 2022). Unlike all these examples, teambuilding activities have as their main characteristic cooperation, increasing the degree of individual participation and training the ability to solve some problems collectively. Thus, it can be stated that collaborative games must represent the very opposite of competition, but the competitive spirit, which inevitably arises, must be speculated and used skilfully. The participants will be directed to compete not with their teammates but with themselves, with an obstacle, with a record (perhaps imaginary), but always with pleasure, without risk. However, when the participants really want to compete, this should not be rejected, being granted as an exception.

Among the suggested suggestions of somewhat "non-competitive" criteria for measuring the success of teambuilding activities, the following can be listed:

- Timing of the duration of the activity—aspect that is transferred to situations at the workplace. Many tasks at the workplace are solved

under conditions of high stress (when deadlines have to be met), highlighting how the participants cope with such situations or how they get involved in solving the task (passive, active, reactive, whatever, non-involvement).
- Reducing the number of participants within the team that must complete the task in a given time.
- The way in which some rules are respected.
- Demonstrations or highlights of rational ways of solving tasks.
- Highlighting the reasons that sometimes prevent the solving of tasks.
- The way in which initiative, creativity were cultivated—highlighting these attributes as often as possible.

1.5.2. Learning different skills and behaviors is done through experimentation

Specialized teambuilding programs are based on the principle of experiential learning (Dewey, 1938; Itin, 1999) according to which learning is effective when people act, discuss what they achieve and the paths to be taken, compare and analyze, develop strategies, test and they discover for themselves the reality and applicability of the knowledge acquired in this way and are not just passive receivers of the transmitted knowledge. It is known that the most lasting method of learning is the one in which the subject experiences the phenomenon and does not just see or hear it.

1.5.3. Promotes personal development with the help of the team

Teambuilding programs facilitate that "empowerment" of the participants, contributing to the increase of self-worth, confidence in oneself and in others, and awareness of the importance of team members' synergy. Self-confidence increases as the individual manages to overcome the imposed challenges (physical-physical or psychological). As he gains the certainty of accomplishing increasingly difficult tasks, the individual feels better, having confidence and courage in overcoming eventual failure, which will lead him to success.

1.5.4. Teambuilding involves everyone's involvement

The programs are designed to involve all participants, possibly by attracting unfavorable reactions from the team whenever a team member shies away from active participation. Within the activities, each member of the team usually has a well-defined role, and in the event of not exercising this role, the team will not be able to complete its tasks.

1.5.5. Teambuilding involves understanding experiences

All challenges are followed by a stage intended for debriefing, analysis, usually by means of the investigation, the way in which it was acted, the similarity with real life, and emphasizing the elements that must be mastered. Thus, an attempt will be made to understand the fundamental principles arising from these experiences and their assimilation (Stefanica & Rosu, 2018). At this stage, the organizer will encourage the participants to explain their reactions and attitudes, launching predetermined questions. In no case will he launch into the analysis of the team's performance.

1.5.6. It includes identifying the potential of the team and individuals

Teambuilding allows the identification of the participants' potential, both as a team, at an organizational level, and as individuals, at an individual level, and establishes the subsequent directions of training and development.

1.5.7. Teambuilding stimulates objective self-evaluation

These programs stimulate the ability to review and evaluate the evolution and own and common behavior, developing the exigency in solving individual and collective tasks.

1.5.8. Facilitates the acquisition of communication and conflict management techniques

As shown by Popescu et al. (2007) in current activities or in the exercise of the service profession, it is necessary to promote, through all possible ways and modalities, a non-conflictual management. "Conflicts must not disrupt the activity of the group in the present or in the future" is the opinion of Dragnea (2006), which implies their eventual mediation and negotiations. Teambuilding can be the ideal mediator of older conflicts between colleagues, offering unexpected opportunities to "delete" the reasons for dissension and move to a stage of full collaboration.

1.5.9. It promotes principles of security, good mood, and voluntary participation

Based on the observance of these principles, the success of the actions is half guaranteed. Assuring the participants about the fact that their performance in the activities is secured and that only they will decide the concrete participation in the actions, all of them seasoned with elements of good mood, will contribute to overcoming fears of any kind and active participation in everything that they undertake. In Figure 1.2, a scenario of a security meeting in the mountain environment is presented.

Figure 1.2. About security.

1.6. The taxonomy of teambuilding

In an attempt to understand the role and place of each means used in teambuilding, we will use their description from the perspective of three basic criteria:

- On the criterion of the external environment: indoor activities and outdoor activities.

- On the criterion of scope of implementation: classic activities (especially those of communication, collaboration, and creation) and adventure or sensational activities, even using extreme sports.
- On the criterion of the sequence of implementation of the forms of activity: introductory, warm-up, "breaking the ice," increasing confidence, cooperation and communication, creativity and inventiveness, fun, and closing.

1.6.1. Indoor activities

These activities take place in the premises; they can be carried out not only as a result of an explicit intention, but also as a result of weather constraints (precipitation, bad weather, too strong sun, etc.). The premises where the activities are carried out can be offered by conference rooms in hotels, dining rooms in mountain huts, or sports halls. Teambuilding organizers must always have alternative solutions for transforming outdoor activities into indoor activities, especially as a result of constraints related to weather conditions.

Usually, these activities combine the sessions of provoked situations with the known means of spending free time in a coordinated and pleasant way.

Due to the fact that a main objective of teambuilding actions is to get employees out of the work environment, that is, out of offices or workshops into nature, indoor activities tend to be considered (rightly) secondary, with outdoor activities being considered the main ones.

Compared to outdoor activities in which physical efforts combined with mental ones predominate, in indoor activities the demands have an inverted weight, predominating the mental ones and to a very small extent the physical ones.

The preferred types of challenge in indoor teambuilding are games or exercises of collaboration-communication, creation, decision-making, and fun. The favorite tools for indoor activities are pen and paper, audio-video presentation tools, and the blackboard. The means associated with indoor are team games, mechanical games, movement activities, skill exercises, cultural-entertaining shows, carnival, etc.

The typical goals of indoor activities can be: establishing a team identity, that is, establishing a name, a slogan, possibly making some objects/accessories to identify the teams, developing an action strategy in which everyone defines and is aware of their role as clear as possible; understanding the work of colleagues by reversing the roles in real life, in which employees with responsibilities and technical skills will become negotiators, and those with sales/marketing specifics will become producers of goods. On this occasion, the employees will become aware of what it means to be in the other's position, increasing empathy and the degree of relationship with work colleagues; establishing a team strategy in challenges with a time limit, conditioning based on rules in solving some situations, etc.; leadership development.

The methodical-organizational indications that must be had in order to organize indoor actions are related to ensuring great attractiveness and interactivity, avoiding continuous writing, dictations, as well as ensuring work comfort by supplementing the activity with informal culinary accessories such as coffee, snacks, sweets, etc.

1.6.2. Outdoor activities

These activities present superior activity possibilities. Among the main reasons why teambuilding is used outside of fires are: favorable weather conditions, the lack of suitable indoor spaces, and the opportunity to carry out special activities that include complex activities through outdoor sports or controlled adventure. Not unimportant is the fact that outdoor activities are designed to provide opportunities for participants to work together in a non-formal and relaxed environment, outside of the usual office space. The outdoors also often involves elements of physical and mental challenge, which can contribute to the development of confidence and team spirit.

The weather can have a significant influence on the planning and execution of an outdoor teambuilding event. The main components of teambuilding influenced by the weather are related to:

- Participant safety: Inclement weather can create hazardous conditions for outdoor activities. For example, heavy rain, storms, excessive heat, or extreme cold may endanger the safety of participants.
- Comfort and mood: Good weather, with sunshine and pleasant temperatures, can contribute to a more relaxed and positive environment, thus increasing the active participation and enthusiasm of team members.
- Accessibility of the location: Bad weather can affect access to the event location, especially in the case of more isolated locations or activities that involve travel.

- Alternative planning: Organizers must have a backup plan for situations in which the weather does not permit outdoor activities. This plan may involve relocating the event to an indoor space or changing planned activities.
- Appropriate equipment: Depending on weather conditions, participants may need additional equipment such as waterproof jackets, footwear suitable for wet or hot conditions, etc.
- Impact on planned activities: Certain activities may be affected by weather conditions. For example, outdoor adventure activities can be dangerous or unpleasant in heavy rain or wind.
- Additional costs: Organizing an outdoor event often involves additional costs to ensure the comfort and safety of participants in the event of adverse weather conditions.

The conditions for organizing outdoor teambuilding activities generate a wide range of examples of activities, among which stand out:

- Creative outdoor workshops: These can include activities such as outdoor painting, sculpture, music, or other forms of artistic expression that encourage creativity and collaboration.
- Outdoor games and competitions: Such activities may involve sports games, team competitions, or other competitive activities that encourage collaboration and team spirit.
- Trust-building experiences: These can involve activities such as adventure parks, obstacle courses, or other physical challenges that require the support and mutual trust of team members.
- Outdoor role-playing or simulations: These can include scenarios where participants must work together to solve specific problems or achieve specific goals.
- Teambuilding with nature adventure challenges: These can include hiking, rock climbing, orienteering, rafting, or other adventure activities that require collaboration and close communication between team members. Such events may involve activities such as building shelter, finding food, and water, orienteering in nature, etc., all of which are designed to develop survival skills and the ability to work

together in extreme situations. As Laşcu (2007) mentions, "routine leads to fatigue and automatism, impoverishes life, decreases the productivity, and creativity of work, as such man must look for remedies, among them finding adventure." Within these challenges, the unforeseen and the dangers can be anticipated and planned, hazard and providence representing attributes that must be avoided by any means. The organization of these programs, however, requires a lot of knowledge on the part of the organizers, but also a very good knowledge and understanding of each participant in the target group, subject to the program.

Types of special activities (different from the classic ones carried out in the form of games) are summarized in the adjacent table (see Table 1.1).

Table 1.1. Special teambuilding activities based on nature adventure and extreme sports

The type of challenge	Brief description	Means used
Adventure in nature	Off-trail walking (trekking) Survival—adventure land	Tents, rucksack, mountain equipment Equipment and food limitations
	Bike adventure	Special bikes—mountain bike
	Horse adventure	Horses, horse-drawn sleighs
	Motorized mobility in nature	Auto-Moto: snowmobiles, ATVs, Off-road
	Imitation of war situations	Weapons of different types: archery, paintball weapons, and airsoft weapons
Extreme sport	Extreme land	Mountaineering, climbing, bouldering, ice climbing, abseiling, zip line, and bungee-jumping
	Extreme water	Rapid rivers, rafting-type boats, kayaking, and recreational kayak
	Extreme air	Skydiving, paragliding, motor paragliding, hot air ballooning, model aircraft, and drones

The description of the particularities of these special programs completes the picture of outdoor activities in which organization and planning play a very important role.

1.6.3. Terrestrial locomotion programs

These programs use in the activity's different means of locomotion such as bicycles, draft animals, motorcycles, and ATVs, as can be seen in Figure 1.3.

Figure 1.3. Locomotive application.

Horseback riding—participants travel on horseback in search of clues that will guide the team to final discoveries. Travel on horses can be replaced by those in a carriage or sleigh, if the activity takes place in winter.

Mountain-biking—represents a type of activity carried out on specially reinforced bicycles to withstand the demands of rugged mountainous terrain. Group trips can use mountain bike trails, mountain roads, paths, and forest roads. The equipment includes the bike, helmet, gloves, raincoat, rucksack of about 20 liters, water tank, bicycle emergency kit, spare tire tube, 1–2 patches, bicycle pump, and flashlight.

Off-road—is defined as transportation with cars capable of moving off mountain roads. The forest roads that cross the mountains in all directions favor the encounter of borderline situations such as a car submerged in mud, adjacent cliffs, and untraveled places.

All-Terrain Vehicle (ATV)—represents those vehicles that can cross different terrains, swamps, sand, mud, in difficult conditions, on mountain paths, or through snow, being very reliable and very safe. These are very suitable for satisfying the spirit of adventure, solving borderline situations, overcoming critical thresholds by all team members, helping, and helping each other.

1.6.4. Types of activities with weapons

Activities with weapons require the observance of strict rules of conduct in the handling of the equipment. The activities take place in polygons specially designed to avoid accidents. Nature offers the possibility of organizing shooting ranges with different weapons, through landforms and not necessarily through infrastructural interventions harmful to the environment. The organization of teambuilding workshops are generally patronized by instructors and performance athletes from shooting sports, in disciplines such as archery or air rifle shooting, darts (throwing with the free hand some objects equipped with needles in order to aim a target located at a variable distance), paintball or airsoft, through scenarios that imitate war situations, representing tools very suitable for teamwork, helping and showing initiative. These types of activity take place in special spaces, especially in forests with varied terrain, or using military constructions and securing territories.

1.6.5. Workshops in the field of mountaineering

Climbing-type activities are used in the sense of increasing individual capacities, increasing self-confidence, and overcoming individual mental barriers, and are less effective in strengthening the team as a whole (Cojanu et al., 2023). However, when such means are used, teammates may first be tasked with training (i.e., how to use the equipment), securing (some difficult areas around the workshops), or guiding (which sockets a colleague should tackle in climbing, or which route would be more accessible on a wall). It is to be avoided that the climbing installations presented are set up by one's own efforts for the realization of teambuilding activities.

Most often, zipline installations are prepared, authorized, and insured in advance and are used for a longer period. Apart from the mentioned workshops, other activities useful for teambuilding can be tackled in the field of mountaineering, but they require access to additional secure locations. From the field of mountaineering, we can distinguish the following workshops: abseiling (descending the rock), climbing (almost vertical climbing on artificial or natural structures), via feratta (approximately lateral crossing of some narrow passages), or the Indian bridge (crossing some streams water on two stretched ropes, on the first placing the feet and on the second the hands), speleological applications (traveling some routes in caves). Examples of these activities can be seen in Figure 1.4.

Figure 1.4. Mountaineering applications.

In all these challenges the team receives additional tasks, by delegating some participants to perform different tasks in support of the team (Derlogea, 2003): to open the way, to secure the group from behind, to transport different equipments, to encourage colleagues, to ensure the physical integrity of colleagues in different situations, to find solutions etc.

1.6.6. Nautical programs

The mountain rivers and lakes provide a suitable setting for various activities related to the means of movement on water, with reference to inflatable boats, motorboats, kayaking, and rafting. Canyoning, known as the activity that defines the passage of canyons formed by mountain waters, without the aid of boats, can also be an interesting challenge for teambuilding, as well as diving to discover the mysteries of wrecks, sunken ruins, or archaeological relics.

1.6.7. Flight programs

Flight programs can be a great choice for a teambuilding event, providing an engaging and challenging experience for participants. Here are some ideas for flight programs that you can include in such an event: glider flight, motor plane flight, tandem skydiving, hot air balloon flight, model aircraft and drone launches, basic piloting courses, and the use of flight simulators.

Regardless of the option chosen, it is important for organizers to ensure that all flight activities are organized and supervised by qualified professionals and that all safety standards are met. This type of experience can build trust and collaboration between team members, giving them a memorable memory and fostering communication and mutual trust.

1.6.8. Winter programs

They are very suitable for teambuilding events and can be full of fun and challenging activities that promote collaboration, communication, and team spirit. Among the ideas of winter outdoor programs for teambuilding, we mention hiking in the snow, constructions in the snow (which especially tests creativity, engineering skills and collaboration), snowmobile adventures, orienteering games, sled races, snowball games, skiing or snowboarding lessons, snowshoeing, and first aid courses in a winter environment. In Figure 1.5, a team begins its mission to find mountain locations based on the clues.

Figure 1.5. Winter application.

Organizers must correctly decipher the weather conditions and have a backup plan in case the weather becomes too difficult for certain activities.

It is also of the utmost importance that all participants are properly equipped to cope with winter conditions.

Within a single teambuilding action, it is important to plan the activities in such a way that there is a logical sequence to achieve the proposed objectives. As in any activity, the unfolding of its moments must support a sequence, or an order, that will ensure the overall success of the activity. The multitude of types of activities presented below, as a rule, excludes the possibility of using them in a single teambuilding action, due to considerations of time, effort made by the participants, the lack of clarity of the purpose of the action, etc. However, to increase the attractiveness of teambuilding actions, a certain diversity of the program is often ensured, respectively, 3–5 distinct types of activities are organized from the classification below, respecting the order presented. Here is a possible sequence of application of the activity forms.

It is important to adapt this sequence to the specific objectives of the teambuilding activity, to the needs and preferences of the group, and to the conditions offered by the location. Organizers will also ensure that there is sufficient time for reflection and discussion to reinforce learnings from the activities.

1.7. Succession of teambuilding activities

Within a single teambuilding action, it is important to plan the activities in such a way that there is a logical sequence of them to achieve the proposed objectives (Derlogea, 2006). As in any activity, the development of its moments must support a sequence, or an order, that will ensure the overall success of the activity.

Here is a possible sequence of application of the forms of activity in teambuilding (see Figure 1.6):

- Warm-up activities and getting to know each other: these are essential in a teambuilding session to help participants feel comfortable and connected with each other. These activities are intended to reduce initial tension and facilitate interaction and communication within the group.
- Trust-building activities between participants: these exercises and games are designed to strengthen bonds between team members, improve communication, and create an environment where participants

Figure 1.6. Succession of team building activities.

feel comfortable working together. These activities are essential for strengthening relationships and creating a sense of team unity.

- Cooperation and collaboration activities: these activities not only encourage collaboration but also develop teamwork skills such as effective communication, mutual trust, active listening, and collective decision-making. These activities encourage participants to work together and achieve common goals.
- Leadership and decision-making activities: in teambuilding and these are crucial because they develop leadership skills and because they improve the decision-making process. These activities encourage participants to assume leadership roles, make strategic decisions, and collaborate towards a common goal.
- Problem-solving activities: the development of problem-solving, collaboration, and communication skills in a team environment is also essential and is carefully targeted in teambuilding. These activities involve challenges or scenarios that require creative thinking, strategy, and innovative approaches to find effective solutions.
- Feedback and reflection activities: they are meant to allow participants to express their thoughts, provide feedback, and evaluate their experience in a constructive way. These activities provide opportunities for self-reflection and generate practical learning that can be applied in the professional environment.

- Relaxation and socializing activities: in teambuilding, they are important because they create a comfortable environment and a relaxing and friendly atmosphere. They strengthen the bonds between participants outside the professional context. These activities facilitate interaction and build stronger relationships between team members.

The multitude of types of activities presented in this book excludes, as a rule, the possibility of using them, as a block, in a single teambuilding action, due to considerations of time, effort made by the participants, the lack of clarity of the purpose of the action, etc. However, in order to increase the attractiveness of teambuilding actions, a certain diversity of the program is often ensured, that is, 3–5 distinct types of activities are organized from the classification below, respecting the order presented.

Bibliography

Cojanu, F., Cătănescu, A., George, N., & Visan, P. (2023). New Ways to Develop Tourism by The Sport Product "Traditional Teambuilding." In E. Soare, & C. Langa (Eds.), Education Facing Contemporary World Issues—EDU WORLD 2022, 5. *European Proceedings of Educational Sciences, 1436–43*. European Publisher. <https://doi.org/10.15405/epes.23045.146>

Deac, V., Bâgu, C. (2000). *Strategia Firmei.* Bucureşti: Editura Eficient.

Derlogea, Ş. (2006). *Teambuilding.* Bucureşti: Editura Amaltea.

Derlogea, Ş. (2003). *Manual de Supravieţuire*. Bucureşti: Editura Amaltea.

Dewey, J. (1938). *Experience & Education*, Kappa Delta Pi, United States, Reprint in 1963 edition by Collier Books, NY.

Douglas, M. (1960). *The Human Side of Enterprise*; Annotated Edition. *McGraw-Hill Professional* (16. Februar 2006).

Dragnea, C. A. (2006). *Elemente de Psihosociologie a Grupurilor Sportive*, Bucureşti: Editura CD Press.

Glover Donald, Midura Daniel (1992). *Teambuilding Through Physical Challenges*. Champaign, IL, USA: Human Kinetics Publishers.

Itin, C. M. (1999). Reasserting the Philosophy of Experiential Education as a Vehicle for Change in the 21st Century. *The Journal of Experiential Education*, *22*(2), 91–8.

Lascu, C. (2007). *Ghidul Turismului de Aventură*. Bucureşti: Editura House of guides.

Maslow, A. H. (1954). *Motivation and Personality*. New York, NY: Harper & Row Publishers.

Popescu, M., Popescu E., & Popescu E. D. (2007), *Managementul Grupurilor de Muncă*. Sibiu: Lucian Blaga.

Rohnke, K., (1989). *Cowstrails and Cobras II-A Project Adventure*. Iowa: Publication in cooperation with Kendall Hunt Publishing Company Dubuque.

Roşca, C., & Roşca D. (2005). *Resurse Umane, Management, Strategii, Politici*. Craiova: Editura Universitaria.

Roşca C., Roşca D., Negulescu M. C., & Neamţu M. (2005). *Resurse Umane—Pregătirea Continuă şi Gestiunea Carierei*. Craiova: Editura Universitaria.

Roşu, D., Cojanu, F., Stefanica, V., & Enache, S. (2022). Experimental Management of Work Collectives through Social and Socialization Activities. *Journal of Physical Education and Sport*, *22*(7), 1742–47. <https://doi/org./10.7752/jpes.2022.07218>.

Suman, G.& Babadag D. (1987). *Alpinism Şcoală a Cutezanţei*. Bucureşti: Editura Militară.

Stefanica, V. & Rosu, R. (2018). Evaluation of the Working Groups in the Group Cohesion Perspective, in the Project Boboc Camp, 2018. *Journal of Physical Education and Sport 18*, 2134. <https://doi/org./10.7752/jpes.2018.s5322>.

Taylor, F. W. (1911). *The Principles of Scientific Management*. Cornell University Library (reprint 24. July 2009).

Todea S. F. (2002). *Jocuri de Mişcare*. Bucureşti: Editura Fundaţiei România de Mâine,

Voicu, V. (2013). *Mediul si Cultura Organizationala în Sport* (The Environment and Organizational Culture in Sport). Pitesti University Publishing House.

CHAPTER 2

Organizational Performance, Knowledge Management, Innovation—Coordinates of Competitive Advantage

Mihaela Diaconu, Daniela Pîrvu, and Amalia Duţu

Summary: This chapter is a theoretical chapter made based on articles published in journals listed/indexed in the most important international databases and establishes the link between teambuilding and organizational performance, respectively the role of knowledge management and innovation transposed in the teambuilding concept as a useful tool in the development of performance in the modern organization. It started dealing with the issue of teambuilding and organizational performance from the fact that, for Romania, it is time for the themes proposed in the teambuilding projects to offer innovative solutions to emerging problems against the background of the anchoring of the national economy in the global economy. The issue of organizational performance treated in the specialized literature was analyzed through multiple dimensions, namely objectives, skills, and development programs. These concepts are developed in this chapter along with organization development programs that contain measures, methods, deadlines, and costs necessary for the development of skills and organizational performance models. Three of the most relevant organizational performance models are presented, namely the McKinsey 7S model, the Nadler-Tushman model, and the Lebas causal performance model, as well as models for evaluating organizational performance relevant in the current context. The motivation for developing organizational performance is presented to ensure long-term success and to maintain the organization's competitiveness and relevance in a constantly changing external environment. Next is presented the concept of knowledge management and organizational innovation, transformational leadership, and organizational learning are presented as variables of organizational performance highlighted within a structural equation model. The concept of open innovation is developed, and the role of individual innovation in supporting organizational competitiveness.

Keywords: Organizational performance, knowledge management, transformational leadership, organizational learning, organizational innovation

2.1. Organizational Performance—Concept and the Need for Development

The issue of organizational performance is complex because organizations present numerous particularities generated by their form, size, field of activity, etc., so that the approach to generalization, in order to create a comprehensive theoretical context, is difficult.

In the context of the multiple challenges that the socio-economic environment addresses to organizations, generated by the intensification of competition and the instability of markets, the issue of organizational performance is being discussed more and more frequently both among researchers and practitioners. Effectively achieving the strategic objectives of organizations, especially those established in the medium and long term, is becoming more and more difficult and organizations must become more and more adaptable to environmental changes. A complex set of indicators is used to assess how well organizations achieve these goals, and the whole process of determining the ability of organizations to achieve and maximize set results is called organizational performance.

In the traditional approach, a company's performance was frequently equated with financial performance.

Shaping the theoretical context for the concept of organizational performance began as early as the 1980s, when researchers concluded that the traditional approach to evaluating an organization's performance based only on financial information was ineffective in accurately describing how the organization achieved its goals (Snow & Hrebiniak, 1980). Law & Wong (1999) highlighted that to properly evaluate the performance of an organization, its multiple dimensions must be taken into account, including the human resource or environment in which the organization develops, as well as the relationships between them.

Over time, numerous authors have contributed to defining the concept of organizational performance. Among them, Chen & Quester (2006) revealed that organizational performance refers to the excellence elements of an organization's managerial and operational activity. Ho (2008) defined organizational performance as an indicator that highlights the extent to which the organization achieves its objectives, being a tool for measuring the quality of management of that organization. Mahapatro (2010) developed this approach, stating that organizational performance is the ability of a company to fulfil its goals and objectives, through effective management that emphasizes good governance and the permanent adaptation of the organization to its environment.

The deepening of the role of the human factor in ensuring organizational performance has generated the emergence of a new concept, called social performance, which over time has come to encompass the various concerns of the organization in the social field, especially related to employees but also to customers, civil society, sustainable development, etc. Numerous authors, including Hillman and Keim (2001), Orlitzky (2008), and Saeidi et al. (2015) demonstrated the existence of a positive relationship between the financial performance and the social performance of the organization.

Currently, organizational performance is a complex concept with multiple dimensions (technical, operational, economic, financial, and social), showing the level of the best results obtained. Considering the need to aggregate the economic, social, and environmental performances of an organization, the notion of global organizational performance must be used.

The dimensions of organizational performance are:

- the objectives;
- the skills;
- the development programs.

Objectives represent quantifiable desired future states for the organization, most of the time in numerical terms. Goals are set for specific periods of time. Long-term goals usually have a planning horizon of more than 5 year. To achieve long-term goals, medium- and short-term goals are formulated. Setting goals correctly and coherently is especially important for the organization because the entire system of organizational relations is built around the goals. At the same time, they are the starting point for planning. The correct and coherent establishment of objectives requires the observance of several principles:

- to be achievable, that is, not to exceed the maximum capabilities available to the organization.
- to be flexible, that is, to allow adjustments, depending on the changes in the environment.
- to be measurable, to enable the process of evaluating the degree to which an objective has been achieved.
- to be specific, that is, clearly indicate what must be achieved, in what time frame, and who is responsible for achieving the objective.
- to be complementary and compatible with the other objectives.

In other words, the organization's objectives must be SMART: Specific, Measurable, Accessible, Relevant, and Timely.

Competencies refer to the specific skills and behaviors that members of the organization and work teams within it must have to contribute effectively to the overall performance and success of the organization. These competencies may be different depending on the nature of the organization, its field of activity, and its specific objectives.

Even if the dimension of organizational performance is determined by many competencies, the most important ones considered as key competencies are:

Communication skills, namely the ability to convey information clearly and effectively, both in written and oral form, and to listen actively.

Teamwork and collaboration between members of the organization, that is, the ability to work well with others and build positive working relationships.

Problem solving and critical thinking, namely the ability to analyze situations, identify problems, and develop effective solutions.

Leadership and management, that is, the ability to lead and inspire others, make decisions, set goals, and manage resources effectively.

Adaptability and flexibility, namely the ability to change approaches or work methods according to circumstances, to learn and manage new situations and challenges.

Innovation and creativity, namely the ability to think creatively, generate new ideas, and contribute to the development of innovative solutions and approaches.

Orientation towards the client/beneficiary, respectively, the ability to understand and satisfy the needs of the organization's clients and/or the beneficiaries of the actions undertaken by the organization.

Time management, namely the ability to prioritize tasks, manage time efficiently, and meet deadlines.

Moral principles and rules of conduct, respectively, the ability to act with integrity, to behave ethically considering the individual interest, not only of the organization as a whole, but also of the organization's external environment.

Conflict resolution, that is, the ability to manage disagreements in a constructive manner, finding solutions acceptable to all parties involved.

Strategic thinking, that is, the ability to think long-term, assess the organization's strengths and weaknesses, identify opportunities and threats, and contribute to the development of strategic plans.

The organization's development programs contain the measures, methods, deadlines, and costs necessary for the development of competences. Two of the most well-known organizational development programs are *Rensis Likert's managerial system* and *the Blake-Mouton organizational development grid.*

In the managerial system developed by the American researcher Rensis Likert, we distinguish four approaches to the development of the organization, differentiated according to the degree of involvement of employees and leaders in the decision-making process, thus:

The explosive system (*exploitative authoritative system)* in which decisions are made centrally by leaders, and employees do not have a significant involvement in the decision-making process. Communication is limited, and working relationships are based on authority and strict control.

The paternalistic system (*benevolent authoritative system*) in which leaders are more open to communication, and decisions are made to a certain extent by consulting employees. The latter have a limited level of autonomy in decision-making.

The consultative system (*consultative system*) in which employees are regularly consulted in the decision-making process. Leaders express interest in employees' opinions and suggestions, but the degree of collaboration and communication is moderate.

The participatory system (*participative system*) in which leaders and employees collaborate closely in the decision-making process, with communication being open and free. Decisions are made collectively, and employees have a high level of involvement and autonomy in managing their activities.

The Blake-Mouton organizational development grid was developed by Robert R. Blake and Jane S. Mouton and addresses two dimensions: leaders' interest in achieving organizational objectives and their attitude towards the needs and interests of employees. Thus, five types of management can be identified that influence the development of the organization (Mora, 2008):

The authoritarian management, oriented exclusively to the achievement of organizational goals, with little interest in the needs and interests of employees. Decisions are made centrally, without considering the opinion or involvement of employees.

The integrative management that strives both to maximize both employee satisfaction and organizational performance, promoting collaboration, and communication.

The indulgent management, which pays high attention to social interactions, needs, and interests of employees and low importance to organizational efficiency.

The minimal management with a low degree of concern both for personnel and for the degree of concern for the achievement of organizational objectives.

The compromise management is concerned with both the achievement of organizational objectives and the needs and interests of employees. Leaders try to create a harmonious and productive work environment.

An organizational performance model is a conceptual framework used to understand, evaluate, and improve organizational performance. Over time, several models of organizational performance have been developed, which can be adapted to the needs of the organization, depending on the field of activity, its purpose, and objectives. Implementing an organizational performance model involves identifying and analyzing the key factors that influence organizational performance. Organizational performance models usually include indicators that help measure and monitor performance over time. Primarily, an effective organizational performance model should provide a comprehensive and detailed picture of the organization's status in relation to its goals, identify strengths and weaknesses, and provide guidance for improving future performance.

According to the authors Bărbulescu & Bâgu (2001), the organizational performance model must relate to:

- the resources necessary for the organization's activity (technical, energetic, material, human, financial).
- work processes carried out within the organization.
- the organizational structure and culture of the organization.
- clients/beneficiaries of the organization (stakeholders).

Among the important organizational models, we mention: the McKinsey 7S model, the Nadler-Tushman Model, and the Lebas causal performance model.

The McKinsey 7S model is a tool that analyzes "organizational design." The purpose of the model is to describe how organizational effectiveness can be achieved through the interactions of seven key elements, which influence each other.

Strategy (**Strategy**), that is, the general plan of the organization to achieve its goals and achieve long-term success.

Structure (**Structure**), respectively, the internal organization of the organization.

System (**System**), with reference to the organizational processes, procedures, and systems that facilitate the current activities of the organization.

Skills (**Skills**), that is, the knowledge, skills, and experience of employees in the organization.

Staff (**Staff**), with reference to the number and categories of employees of the organization.

Style (**Style**), with reference to how decisions are made, communicated, and interactions are managed in the organization.

Shared values (**Shared values**), that is, the fundamental beliefs and principles that are shared by the members of the organization.

The McKinsey 7S model is used to help organizations analyze the current state and plan strategic changes to improve organizational performance and effectiveness.

The Nadler-Tushman model is centered on the analysis of organizational systems and the identification of factors that can influence the organization's performance in various contexts and situations.

Organizational performance is seen as the result of the effective interaction and integration of several organizational subsystems, namely organizational structure, technology, organizational culture, processes, staff, and the external environment.

The model identifies three main components of an organizational system that must be harmonized in order to optimize organizational performance. These components are:

The input component comprises all the resources (e.g., people, technology, capital, raw materials) and environmental factors that enter the organization and can influence performance.

The process component refers to how input resources are transformed into products, services, or outputs in the organization. Organizational processes, including workflows, communication, decisions, and interactions, are critical to organizational performance.

The output component refers to the products, services, or results, including financial, that are generated by the organization and that are directed to the external environment.

Any discrepancy or dysfunction in one of the above components can negatively affect organizational performance. Therefore, analyzing, and correcting discrepancies between input, process, and output components is essential to improve organizational performance.

The Lebas causal performance model analyzes the causal relationships between the factors that influence organizational performance, namely financial aspects, human resources, technology, strategy, organizational culture, processes, management systems, and other internal and external factors. By using this model, organizations can identify the critical factors influencing their performance and make more informed decisions to develop more effective strategies to achieve organizational goals.

Performance evaluation is necessary because, through this, organizations can establish the extent to which the objectives have been achieved and develop future initiatives in order to improve their performance.

Organizational performance can be evaluated considering several criteria, including operational efficiency, strategic effectiveness, customer satisfaction, employee engagement and satisfaction, innovation, quality of products or services, financial indicators, etc. Ghalayini and Noble (1996) consider that the evaluation of the organization's performance is a process with a regular character, through which the results are measured, and which is based on the use of a multidimensional set of indicators. Most specialists link the evaluation of the organization's performance to the concepts of efficiency and effectiveness (Neely et al., 1995; Melnyk et al., 2014; Mura et al., 2021).

Organizational performance appraisal usually includes:

- **The operational performance** involves evaluating how well the organization carries out its current activities to achieve its objectives. Operational performance includes an assessment of marketing, customer satisfaction, product quality, market share, sales volume, and competitive advantage. Operational performance can be evaluated according to:

- The efficiency of the processes, making assessments regarding the reduction of costs, the increase of productivity, the minimization of losses and waste, etc.
- The quality of the products and services provided is measured by standards, norms, and customer/beneficiary feedback.
- Flexibility and quick reaction to changes, which assesses the organization's ability to respond quickly to customer/beneficiary requirements and adapt to new trends and market conditions.

- The financial performance by which the size of revenues and profit margins is evaluated. Financial performance can be revealed through liquidity, solvency, profitability, return on assets, etc. Financial performance is an assessment of the organization's financial condition and its performance in the context of established objectives. A healthy financial performance can provide the organization with the necessary resources for future investment, innovation, and growth, as well as to meet unforeseen financial challenges.
- The capital performance refers to how the organization uses and manages the different types of capital it has available to achieve its objectives and create value for all stakeholders (such as shareholders, customers, employees, and the community). Assessing capital performance is important for ensuring sustainable organizational performance. These types of capital include:

The financial capital, such as own funds, loans, revenues, and profits. The performance of financial capital is essential for evaluating the organization's ability to generate profits or added value and to finance future investments.

The intellectual capital includes the knowledge, skills, and abilities of the organization's employees, as well as intellectual property, patents, and know-how. The performance of intellectual capital is related to the organization's ability to innovate, develop quality products or services, and maintain its competitive advantage in the market.

The structural capital refers to the structure and efficiency of the organization's systems, processes, and procedures, as well as the quality of relationships with customers, suppliers, and business partners. The performance of the structural capital is evaluated by the level of optimization of the operational processes.

The relational capital involves the organization's relationships and collaborations with external stakeholders such as customers, suppliers, business partners, and the community. Relational capital performance is related to customer loyalty, customer satisfaction, and the organization's contribution to community development and social responsibility.

The natural capital refers to the natural resources and the environment, which the organization uses in its activities. Natural capital performance involves the organization's commitment to sustainability, protecting the environment, and responsible use of natural resources.

Among the organizational performance evaluation models, established in the specialized literature, we mention:

The Balanced Scorecard Model (**BSC**), developed by Robert Kaplan and David Norton that allows measuring organizational performance in four key areas: financial, internal processes, customers, and organizational learning/growth. The BSC is based on the idea that the performance of the organization should not only be evaluated according to financial indicators, but also according to other key aspects that contribute to the success of the organization. These perspectives are divided into four main categories:

The important financial perspective for the organization's shareholders/owners, employees, creditors, suppliers, etc. refers to the measurement of the organization's performance based on financial aspects (revenues, profits, costs, investments, etc.).

The customer/beneficiary perspective focuses on meeting the needs of customers/beneficiaries. Indicators in this category may include the degree of customer/beneficiary satisfaction, market share, level of customer/beneficiary loyalty, their feedback, etc.

The internal processes perspective refers to the organization's internal processes and operations. Indicators in this category may include operational efficiency, product quality, production time, operational costs, etc.

The personal and innovation perspective focuses on the issue of human resources. Indicators in this category may include the level of knowledge of employees, the ease of communication between employees, the degree of innovation, the use of advanced technologies, etc.

The EFQM model (**European foundation for quality management**) assesses the performance of organizations in a wide range of areas, including leaders, strategy and planning, processes, human resources, partnerships, and organizational resources. The model uses a comprehensive set of criteria and practices that help organizations assess and improve their performance in a systematic and sustainable way. The nine fundamental criteria of the EFQM model are divided into two main categories: "Results" and "Driver factors."

The "Results" criteria are:
Customer/beneficiary results that measure customer/beneficiary satisfaction and loyalty, as well as the organization's impact on its customers.

Staff results relate to employee engagement, professional development, and performance, as well as the organization's impact on staff wellbeing.

Society results that measure the organization's contribution to society's well-being, including aspects related to sustainability, social responsibility, and community impact.

Key process results evaluate the level of quality, efficiency, and innovation in the organization.

The "Driver factors" are:
Leadership and governance assess how the organization's leaders set the organization's strategic directions, create a culture of excellence, and ensure effective governance.

Strategy and planning, which refers to how the organization develops and implements strategies, plans, and tactics to achieve objectives and adapt to environmental changes.

Resource management, which assesses how the organization manages human, financial, and physical resources to achieve its objectives and improve its performance.

Process management that focuses on how the organization optimizes and improves internal processes and operations to deliver quality products and services.

Partnership and resource management that assesses relationships with partners, suppliers, and other stakeholders and how they contribute to the organization's performance.

The Malcolm Baldrige National Quality Award Model, it is centered on several key criteria, known as the Criteria for Organizational Performance and Excellence, which are periodically updated to reflect changes in the business environment and customer/beneficiary expectations. The criteria are divided into seven main categories:

Leadership with reference to the ability to guide, motivate, and influence people to achieve the organization's objectives and to achieve its mission in an efficient and effective manner.

Strategy with reference to the long-term strategic approaches developed to guide the organization in achieving its objectives and in achieving its mission, in close connection with the challenges generated by the external environment.

Customers evaluate how the organization fulfils its commitments to customers, measures customer satisfaction, and improves their experience.

Measurement, Analysis, and Knowledge Management, which assesses how the organization measures performance, analyzes data and information, and uses knowledge to support decisions and improve its processes and results.

Workforce which assesses how the organization invests in employee development, engagement, and well-being, as well as a culture of diversity and inclusion.

Operations that assess how the organization designs, manages, and improves processes to deliver its products and services with quality and efficiency.

Results which evaluate the organization's performance in terms of financial and market results, customer satisfaction, employee engagement, social impact, etc.

Developing organizational performance is critical to the success and sustainability of an organization in an increasingly competitive and rapidly changing external environment. Some key reasons why the development of organizational performance is important, as it results from the analysis of the specialized literature (Senge, 1991; Ries, 2017; Collins and Collins, 2021; Afzal & Lim, 2022; Dong, 2023; Dimas et al., 2023) are revealed below:

Increasing competitiveness. By improving the quality of products or services, optimizing processes, and quickly adapting to market changes, organizations can gain a competitive advantage.

Increasing customer satisfaction. Organizations that deliver quality products and services, meet delivery deadlines, quickly and efficiently solve potential problems reported by customers, and personalize the customer buying experience have more satisfied customers who are likely to return to the products/services offered and remain loyal to the organization.

The development of organizational performance involves the identification and elimination of dysfunctions or non-conformities in organizational processes. Thus, the organization can save time and resources, leading to increased efficiency and lower costs.

Motivating employees can lead to an engaged, creative, and productive workforce, with direct and immediate impact on the development of organizational performance.

Increasing innovation and adaptability enable organizations to remain relevant and competitive in the long term.

Effective risk management. Well-managed organizations can identify, assess, and manage risks to minimize their impact on activities and results.

Increasing credibility and reputation in front of customers, business partners, investors, and employees.

Ensuring long-term sustainability and growth of the organization, whereby the organization can experience sustainable growth and remain viable in the future.

Therefore, developing organizational performance is crucial to ensure long-term success and to maintain the organization's competitiveness and relevance in an ever-changing external environment.

2.2. Knowledge management and innovation, variables of strategic competitive advantage

In the current context, organizations place knowledge and informational resources in a strategic position. Information, knowledge management is considered an activity aimed at ensuring organizational performance through organizational innovation and transformational leadership. Knowledge is defined by researchers as a set of concepts, ideas, rules, and procedures that guide actions and decisions (Emadzade et al., 2012). This set is considered an integrative system within which organizational activities are coordinated, through which needs are identified of knowledge and establish the actions through which knowledge is acquired, understood, transferred, and used to achieve the organizational objectives, through which the organization will become high performing. Through knowledge management, the transfer of theoretical knowledge to practical activity is achieved and thus value is given to them with impact positively on organizational transformation.

Allameh & Abbas (2010) classified knowledge into three levels:

1. Basic knowledge: minimum amount of knowledge that is necessary to complete the teaching process.
2. Advanced knowledge: knowledge that helps organizations to be competitive to have their own knowledge.
3. Innovative knowledge: knowledge that enables organizations to govern their industry and competitors.

Knowledge management and organizational innovation, transformational leadership, and organizational learning are considered by Ali Noruzy s.a. (2013) as variables of organizational performance and are highlighted within a structural equation model. According to the study of the cited authors, organizational learning influences organizational performance directly and indirectly through knowledge management and organizational innovation, and organizational innovation influences organizational performance through good knowledge management.

Knowledge management is a concept that highlights the set of tools with which knowledge is managed so that it brings value within the organization to achieve performance and competitive advantage. It is considered a strategic element within most large companies, as the value of the company is influenced by its ability to create and manage knowledge to achieve organizational performance by obtaining a sustainable competitive advantage and innovation. An important advantage of knowledge management is not only the facilitation of collaboration in the process of innovation, but also identifying the difference between the basic knowledge and the remedies to blur the differences. It also supports the development of a culture of innovation within the organizational culture. Studies have highlighted that middle managers are considered the knowledge creators who make the link between top managers and front-line managers, and therefore are the ones who could effectively manage knowledge management to create innovation.

From the study carried out by Nawab et al. (2015) it is found that the specific processes of knowledge management, namely knowledge creation, knowledge organization, knowledge storage, knowledge sharing and knowledge use contribute to the improvement of innovation, therefore the key success factors of knowledge management are: Management leadership and support, Organizational culture, Knowledge Management strategy, Removal of resource constraints, Processes and activities, Human resource management, Organizational infrastructure, Performance measurement, Training and education, Information technology, Rewarding and motivation, and Benchmarking (Changiz, 2010).

Transformational leadership is seen as a managerial style by which employees are motivated and intellectually stimulated through charismatic discourse. Seaver (2010) defined transformational leadership as a leadership style in which leaders and employees stimulate themselves to achieve high levels of motivation and morality within their own organization. This style is promoted by leaders who manage to create an atmosphere of trust within the organization that stimulates employees to achieve higher performance than expected. It is based on changes in beliefs, on the needs and values of the parties involved in the process. Al-Hakim (2011) believes that leadership is an important critical success factor of knowledge management and is also useful in implementing knowledge management as a support to achieve the highest level of organizational performance.

Organizational learning is defined by Templeton s.a. (2002) as the set of actions (knowledge acquisition, information distribution, information interpretation, and organizational memory) within the organization that intentionally and unintentionally influence positive organizational change and is considered to have an important role in the context of strategic management as a source of competitive advantage (Zollo & Winter, 2002). Creating a team, establishing a change strategy are activities carried out by the transformational leader to create an environment of organizational learning.

Organizational experience, cognitive processes, acquisition, knowledge exchange, and their use are variables that contribute to the development of organizational learning and organizational performance as a source of competitive advantage. Leaders of organizations have an important role in facilitating organizational learning by becoming transformative leaders capable of developing teams, establishing the trajectory of change for achieving performance (Berson et al., 2006).

Alrubaiee et al. (2015) conducted a study in which they investigated the mediating effect of organizational innovation on the relationship between knowledge, management processes, and organizational performance. The result of the study confirmed the strong positive effect of knowledge management processes on innovation and organizational performance, as well as the positive effect of organizational innovation on the relationship between knowledge management processes and organizational performance. The model created in the study is presented in Figure 2.1.

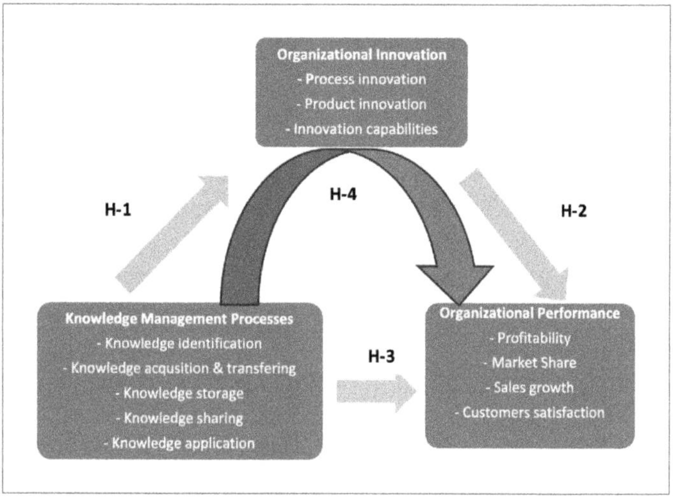

Figure 2.1. The conceptual model. After: Alrubaiee et al. (2015), *International Review of Management and Business Research* 4(4), 995.

The results of the quoted study are consistent with previous empirical studies quoted by the authors of the study, namely Noruzy et al. (2013); Darroch (2005); Marques et al. (2014); Tsai & Shih (2004); Holm & Sharma (2006); Akroush & Al-Mohammad (2010); Hanvanich et al. (2003; 2006).

The results of the study are also similar to those studies that show a positive effect of knowledge management processes on organizational performance (Tubigi & Alshawi, 2015; Al-Hakm & Hassan, 2012). Also, the authors' findings confirm the result of previous empirical studies cited by the authors that found a positive effect of organizational innovation on organizational performance (Marques et al., 2014; Han et al., 1998; Agarwal et al., 2003; Hult et al., 2004; Zheng et al., 2005; Farhangmehr et al., 2006; Keskin, 2006; Alrubaiee et al., 2013). In addition to the mentioned studies, the authors of the conceptual model identified the mediating effect of organizational innovation on the relationship between knowledge management processes and organizational performance.

Human resources play a strategic role in the evolution of the organization and in achieving performance. The practices in the field of strategic management must be thought of in such a way that they coincide with the specifics of the organizational culture and determine organizational competitiveness. Within the framework of complementary practices in the field of HR, an important role belongs to the stimulation of product/service innovation as a performance indicator. In the innovation process, creating an appropriate climate based on the culture of quality, as well as stimulating creativity through human resources policies, are strategic activities.

The authors Lau and Ngo (2004, p. 686) presented three sets of HR practices that have been highlighted in the literature that would support an innovation-oriented HR system. They are: (1) training-focused—an emphasis on skills enhancement and human capital investment; (2) performance-based reward—an emphasis on rewarding employees' contributions and outcomes; and (3) team development—leadership and team-based activities are extensively developed and carried out. In particular, a cross-functional team is often suggested as a critical organizational tool. In their study, the cited authors concluded that organizational culture plays a mediating role between human resources and the organization's ability to achieve results in the field of innovation. Human resource training, rewards, and teamwork are determining factors in the process of organizational innovation to achieve competitiveness.

Individual innovation plays an important role in achieving organizational goals. It can be defined as the willingness of an individual to try new things, to have a positive perspective towards innovation in pursuit of benefit. Since organizations must have information and collaborations to innovate processes, products, and services to support competitiveness, the concept of open innovation appeared in specialized literature and is addressed with particular interest. Open innovation involves both internalization activities of new ideas that come to the firm, but also internally developed ideas that are oriented to the external environment. Kumar Singh et al. (2021) in the study entitled "Top management knowledge value, knowledge sharing practices, open innovation and organizational performance" highlighted the fact that top management has a critical role in terms of valuing knowledge and their sharing practices to support open innovation. They also emphasized that open innovation influences the organizational performance of SMEs, although in the literature, there are few studies on the link between open innovation and organizational performance. Other authors highlight the link between organizational flexibility (Hienerth et al., 2011), organizational culture and employee characteristics (Appu & Sia, 2017; Della Peruta et al., 2016; Huizingh, 2011), the innovation climate (Popa et al., 2017; Sia & Appu, 2015) and innovation strategy (Burnswicker & Vanhaverbeke, 2015) that have an impact on open innovation. The effect of leaders and their directions (West et al., 2003), along with knowledge sharing practices (Del Giudice et al. 2015; Shujahat et al., 2019), play critical roles in open innovation. Therefore, the authors of the study believe that knowledge sharing stimulates innovation (Calantone & Stanko, 2007; Khedhaouria & Jamal, 2015; Lin, 2007; Tangaraja et al., 2015) and that top management support is necessary for knowledge sharing practices (Lin, 2007).

Bibliography

Allameh, S. M., & Abbas, S. K. (2010). The Relationship between Knowledge Management Practices and Innovation Level in Organizations: Case Study of Sub-companies of Selected Corporations in the City of Esfahan. *Journal of Business Case Studies (JBCS)*, *6*(1).

Alrubaiee, L. S., Al-zu'bi, H., Hanandeh, R., & Ali, R. (2015). Investigating the Relationship Between Knowledge Management Processes and Organizational Performance the Mediating Effect of Organizational Innovation. *International Review of Management and Business Research 4*, 989.

Afzal, F., & Lim, B. (2022). Organizational Factors Influencing the Sustainability Performance of Construction Organizations. *Sustainability 14*(16), 10449.

Berson, Y., Nemanich, L. A., Waldman, D. A., Galvin, B. M., & Keller, R. T. (2006). Leadership and organizational learning: A multiple levels perspective. *The leadership quarterly 17*(6), 577–94.

Chen, S. C., & Quester, P. G. (2006). Modeling Store Loyalty: Perceived Value in Market Orientation Practice. *Journal of Services marketing 20*(3), 188–98.

Cristina, M. O. R. A. (2008). Leadership și dezvoltare organizațională în administrația publică locală din România. *Revista Transilvană de Științe Administrative 10*(21), 29–46

Dimas, I. D., Torres, P., Rebelo, T., & Lourenço, P. R. (2023). Paths to Team Success: A Configurational Analysis of Team Effectiveness. *Human Performance*, 1–25.

Dong, B. (2023). A Systematic Review of the Organizational Inertia Literature and Future Outlook. *International Journal of Education and Humanities 8*(2), 119–23.

Emadzade, M. K., Mashayekhi, B., & Abdar, E. (2012). Knowledge Management Capabilities and Organizational Performance. *Interdisciplinary Journal of Contemporary Research in Business 3*(11), 781–90.

Hassan, S., & Al-Hakim, L. A. Y. (2011). The Relationships Among Critical Success Factors of Knowledge Management, Innovation and Organizational Performance: A Conceptual Framework. In *2011 International Conference on Management and Artificial Intelligence*, pp. 94–103.

Hillman, A. J., & Keim, G. D. (2001). Shareholder Value, Stakeholder Management, and Social issues: What's the Bottom Line? *Strategic Management Journal 22*(2), 125–39.

Ho, L. A. (2008). What Affects Organizational Performance? The Linking of Learning and Knowledge Management. *Industrial Management & Data Systems 108*(9), 1234–54.

Kaplan, R. S., & Norton, D. P. (1992). Measures That Drive Performance. *Harvard Business Review.*

Kurtipek, S., & Güngör, N. (2019). Individual Innovation: A Research on Sports Manager Candidates. *Journal of Education and Learning.*

Lau, C. M., & Ngo, H. Y. (2004). The HR System, Organizational Culture, and Product Innovation. *International Business Review 13*(6), 685–703.

Law, K. S., & Wong, C. S. (1999). Multidimensional Constructs M Structural Equation Analysis: An Illustration Using the Job Perception and Job Satisfaction Constructs. *Journal of Management 25*(2), 143–60.

Mahapatro, B. B. (2022). *Human Resource Management*. PG Department of Business Management.

Nawab, S., Nazir, T., Zahid, M. M., & Fawad, S. M. (2015). Knowledge Management, Innovation and Organizational Performance. *International Journal of Knowledge Engineering 1*(1), 43–8.

Noruzy, A., Dalfard, V. M., Azhdari, B., Nazari-Shirkouhi, S., & Rezazadeh, A. (2013). Relations Between Transformational Leadership, Organizational Learning, Knowledge Management, Organizational Innovation, and Organizational Performance: An Empirical Investigation of Manufacturing Firms. *The International Journal of Advanced Manufacturing Technology 64*, 1073–85.

Orlitzky, M. (2008). Corporate Social Performance and Financial Performance: A Research Synthesis. In Andrew Crane et al. (eds), *The Oxford Handbook of Corporate Social Responsibility*, Oxford Academic.

Ries, E. (2011). The Lean Startup: How Today's Entrepreneurs Use Continuous Innovation to Create Radically Successful Businesses. *Currency*.

Saeidi, S. P., Sofian, S., Saeidi, P., Saeidi, S. P., & Saaeidi, S. A. (2015). How Does Corporate Social Responsibility Contribute to Firm Financial Performance? The Mediating Role of Competitive Advantage, Reputation, and Customer Satisfaction. *Journal of Business Research 68*(2), 341–50.

Seaver, D. S. (2000). Effect of Transformational Leadership in a Cross-Cultural Organization: A Case Study. Capella University.

Senge, P. M. (2006). The Fifth Discipline: The Art and Practice of the Learning Organization. *Broadway Business*.

Singh, S. K., Gupta, S., Busso, D., & Kamboj, S. (2021). Top Management Knowledge Value, Knowledge Sharing Practices, Open innovation and Organizational Performance. *Journal of Business Research 128*, 788–98.

Snow, C. C., & Hrebiniak, L. G. (1980). Strategy, Distinctive Competence, and Organizational Performance. *Administrative Science Quarterly*, 317–36.

Spear, S. J. (2009). *High-Velocity Edge: How Market Leaders Leverage Operational Excellence to Beat the Competition*. McGraw-Hill Education.

Templeton, G. F., Lewis, B. R., & Snyder, C. A. (2002). Development of a Measure for the Organizational Learning Construct. *Journal of Management Information Systems 19*(2), 175–218.

Valmohammadi, C. (2010). Identification and Prioritization of Critical Success Factors of Knowledge Management in Iranian SMEs: An Experts' View. *African Journal of Business Management 4*(6), 915–24.

Zollo, M., & Winter, S. G. (2002). Deliberate Learning and the Evolution of Dynamic Capabilities. *Organization Science 13*(3), 339–51.

CHAPTER 3

Teambuilding Programs—Determinants, Characteristics, Effects, Integrated Approach: Organization, Team, Individual

Amalia Duţu, Mihaela Diaconu, and Bogdan Georgescu

Summary: The literature presents teambuilding as a type of activity designed to break down individual psychological barriers, increase cohesion between team members, and create a more efficient and productive working environment. This chapter aimed to identify the factors determining the effects of teambuilding programs and how to evaluate the results, using a three-pronged approach: ORGANIZATION, TEAM, and EMPLOYEE. A mixed research methodology—focus group and survey—was used to achieve this aim. All groups interested in the design and implementation of teambuilding programs—HR specialists, managers, organizational psychologists—participated in the research. The chapter is organized into two parts. The first part presents the results of the focus groups that formed the basis for the design of the structured questionnaire. The second part presents the results of the survey that aimed to measure the degree of importance of the antecedents and effects of teambuilding programs and to identify their variability according to the size of the company and the level at which it operates—national versus international.

Keywords: Teambuilding, determinants, effects, organizational performance, measuring effects, national companies, international companies

The present study aimed to identify the determinants, characteristics, and effects of teambuilding programs, the analysis being conducted from an approach that integrates three perspectives—ORGANIZATION, TEAM, and INDIVIDUAL. Thus, the main research questions underlying this study were:

- What are the factors that determine the characteristics of a teambuilding program?
- To what extent does the degree of importance of the determined factors vary according to organizational characteristics—size, level of operation (national, international).
- What are the characteristics of a successful teambuilding program? How should a successful teambuilding program be designed?
- What are the effects of teambuilding programs on the organization? What about the employee? When should we measure these effects and with what tools?

Both qualitative and quantitative methods were selected to answer these research questions.

3.1. 360° analysis of the concept of teambuilding in order to identify—determinants, characteristics, and effects. Understanding the links between teambuilding and different organizational variables

Three focus groups were conducted in the research process, involving three groups interested in the design and implementation of teambuilding programs: (1) human resources specialists (responsible for the implementation of teambuilding programs in organizations); (2) psychologists with expertise in organizational psychology (theorists and researchers); and (3) managers (top-management)—decision makers in the allocation of teambuilding budgets/funders of teambuilding programs. Thus, a 360° analysis of the teambuilding concept was carried out in order to identify—determinants, characteristics, effects, links between teambuilding, and different organizational variables.

3.1.1. Sampling procedures

35 participants were recruited to participate in the focus groups. Participants were identified by convenience sampling and snowball sampling. In the first stage, up to five participants from each group were recruited to participate in focus group discussions in groups of 9–12 participants. Initially recruited participants were given the opportunity to invite other experts in the field (recruited from the professional networking network) to contact the research team to participate.

3.1.2. Data collection

Data were collected between June and July 2023 using communication platforms (Zoom and Skype). Discussions were audio recorded. The average duration of a focus group was approximately 50 min. The focus group guide used was customized for each group as follows:

(I) Psychologists specializing in organizational psychology

The focus group guide contained five discussion themes related to a better understanding of teambuilding perceptions—(1) identifying the characteristics of teambuilding programs with high effect on effectiveness (individual, organizational); (2) identifying the factors that determine the characteristics of a teambuilding program; (3) understanding the links that exist between teambuilding programs and a number of individual variables; (4) understanding the links that exist between teambuilding programs and a number of organizational variables; (5) identifying the effects of teambuilding programs at organizational and individual level; and (6) concretely how these effects can be measured and with what tools.

Focus group guide:

1. What is your general opinion about teambuilding?
2. I invite you to make a list of the factors that determine the characteristics of a teambuilding program/product.
3. What are the effects of teambuilding on the employees of a company/institution? What about the organization? Please make an inventory of the effects from this double perspective: individual (employee) and organization.
4. Considering the employee's perspective, what do you think is the link between teambuilding and the following individual variables: attachment to the organization, willingness to leave the organization, loyalty to the organization, stress level, work motivation, individual effectiveness, cognitive abilities (attention, motivation and goal setting, creativity, perception, behavior management, anticipation and planning, etc.).
5. If we look at it from an individual perspective, what do you think should be the characteristics of a teambuilding product that generates individual performance growth? What about from an organizational perspective?
6. How can we measure the impact of teambuilding programs on individual performance? What about organizational performance? What tools/methods can we use for this purpose?

(II) Managers, HR managers, and HR specialists

The focus group guide contained five discussion themes related to better understanding perceptions of teambuilding—(1) identifying characteristics of teambuilding programs with high effect on effectiveness (individual, organizational); (2) understanding the links that exist between teambuilding programs and a number of individual variables; (3) understanding the links that exist between teambuilding programs and a number of organizational variables; (4) identifying the effects of teambuilding programs at organizational and individual level; and (5) concretely how these effects can be measured and with what tools.

Focus group guide:

1. What is your general opinion about teambuilding?
2. Is teambuilding for all departments or only for some departments? Is it more effective from a results perspective to be organized intra-departmentally or inter-departmentally? Is teambuilding a cost or an investment?
3. Based on your experience, please explain the link between teambuilding and individual performance, organizational performance, and organizational culture?
4. I invite you to make a list of factors that determine the characteristics of a teambuilding program/product.
5. Please list the effects of teambuilding programs on employees (individual and team perspective) and on the company as a whole.
6. How can we measure the impact of teambuilding programs on individual performance? What tools/methods can we use for this purpose?

3.1.3. Data analysis

Group discussions were transcribed using MAXQDA. In the first round of coding, the aim was to identify the determinants, characteristics, and effects of the teambuilding programs, while considering possible relationships that were not part of the original project design. To this end, the analysis was initially carried out with four a priori codes reflecting the four topics of the interview guides. These topics were; (1) general perceptions of teambuilding programs; (2) factors that determine the characteristics of a teambuilding program; (3) links between teambuilding programs and certain individual and organizational variables; (4) effects of teambuilding programs; (5) impact evaluation/measuring effects—how? With what tools?; and (5) surprising. The “surprising” code allowed the identification of some issues that were not considered in the initial design stage of the focus group guide. In the second stage of coding, in each previously constituted category, outcomes that appear to be patterns, and those outcomes that appear to deviate significantly from the patterns were identified. In the third stage, based on the results, conceptual models were developed—Antecedents and effects of teambuilding programs—an integrated approach: organizational and individual; Stages of designing and implementing teambuilding programs.

3.1.4. Results and discussions

Based on the data analysis procedures described in the section above, the analysis reached consensus on four themes. The first theme was GENERAL PERCEPTIONS of teambuilding programs. Participants shared their experiences of teambuilding programs, their views on what these programs represent. The second theme was BACKGROUND OF TEAMBUILDING PROGRAMS. Participants discussed the different organizational, team, and individual characteristics that have a significant impact on the construction and implementation of a teambuilding program. The third theme was the effects of TEAMBUILDING PROGRAMS. Participants reported, based on their personal experiences, the different effects that teambuilding programs have on the organization, the team, and the employees and detailed how these effects were observed, thus identifying the links between teambuilding programs and different organizational and individual variables. The fourth theme was MEASURING/EVALUATING the impact of teambuilding programs.

3.1.4.1. General perceptions of teambuilding programs

- In general, teambuilding programs were perceived differently by focus group participants. However, participants tended to see the teambuilding program either as a tool available to the organization or as a context developed by the organization for different purposes, such as:
  1. development tools at both the individual and team level;
  2. tool for increasing organizational/individual effectiveness/performance;
  3. tool for organizational culture development/change;
  4. a tool for organizational and team member alignment;
  5. a tool with broad application across all fields/industries and all types of companies;

6. a tool that is applied in a particular way according to the characteristics and goals of the organization;
7. with adaptation and customization;
8. a tool whose use at the level of the organization is related to the management mindset and not necessarily to the budget;
9. a short-term cost, a long-term investment;
10. a context of discovery and self-discovery;
11. a context of bonding between new and old colleagues;
12. a context of sharing feelings/emotions with colleagues;
13. a context of repositioning within the group;
14. a context for developing organizational/group/individual mindsets;
15. an informal/semi-formal context of repositioning/validation of roles within teams;
16. a context of discovering/rediscovering colleagues, boss, management, etc.
17. a context to increase connection and bonds within the group;
18. a context of getting out of the stress zone and routine;
19. a context of organizational freedom.

- When it comes to the ideal form of teambuilding programs from an organizational perspective—interdepartmental versus single-departmental/team—participants reported that this is variable depending on the goals and objectives of the organization:

> "… there is no formula for success, it depends on the objectives, purpose, budget, and other aspects of the organisation …"

> "… would go for interdepartmental teambuilding, that is, participants from several departments, but of course it depends on what management is aiming for …"

> "… probably multiple departments would be ideal, but clearly it can be just one department/one team … depends on what is being pursued …"

> "we have implemented organized programs and interdepartmentally, but also at team level."

- When it comes to how teambuilding programs should be organized with or without family members, participants tend to feel that they should be limited to the presence of members of the organization:

> "… family has no place in teambuilding programs …"

"When you participate in a teambuilding program it is an opportunity to spend time with colleagues ..."

"Teambuilding is not a trip, it doesn't have to involve family..."

"I think that the presence of family no longer gives you the opportunity to spend time with colleagues and to connect emotionally with them for the simple reason that you tend to focus your attention on family members..."

- Opinions are aligned on the place of the psychologist in the design and implementation of teambuilding programs. Both managers, HR specialists, and especially psychologists appreciate that:

"... the first to intervene in the design of a teambuilding program should be the psychologist who should do a needs analysis at group and individual level ..."

"... the psychologist is where it starts ..."

"... psychologist should identify problems and conflicts within the group, communication barriers ..."

"I want happy and fulfilled people in the company. I know this will be reflected in the company's performance. We work outsourced with a specialist firm that helps us to identify employee/team needs and issues. And, yes, you can see the results ..."

"When I participated in a teambuilding program, there was a psychologist on the team. Along the way, he helped us to identify communication barriers and blockages between us, the participants, and helped us to communicate openly with each other ..."

"The psychologist should be part of the team implementing the teambuilding program, he is also important in the process of measuring the results."

- The most important objectives of teambuilding programs, according to participants' experiences, are:
  1. Implementation of organizational change programs;
  2. Organizational redesign, validation of new roles;
  3. Role redefinition;
  4. Aligning teams to common objectives, goals;
  5. Uniting teams, increasing cohesion, improving communication;
  6. Increasing performance across the organization;
  7. Increasing team performance;
  8. Increase attachment to the organization, improve employer brand.

3.1.4.2. Determinants of teambuilding programs

When it comes to the factors that determine the characteristics of a teambuilding program, participants say that they are related to both the organization and the individual.

- Characteristics of the organization—industry, size, internal structure, geographical spread of operations (national/international), etc.

"It clearly depends on what the company does, how big it is and what industry it's in. Each company, depending on these aspects, sets the details of its teambuilding programs. I mean, if a hotel and another is when you produce cars …"

"No question that a large company implements different types of programs compared to small companies. If the company has only 10 employees, probably programs are run with all employees, whereas a company with 1000 employees develops and implements programs organized by goals, groups …"

- Management mindset

"Teambuilding is clearly determined by the management mindset and how the manager sees and understands the use of this tool …"

"Teambuilding is determined first by the mindset of the management and then by the budget."

"In the Romanian company, at least, we are clearly talking about the mentality of the management which influences the budget allocation for teambuilding and its use …"

"Teambuilding is, after all, part of the organizational culture and this is shaped by management mentality."

- Budget allocated to the teambuilding program

"The budget we have at our disposal dictates what and how we do, organizing teambuilding programs"

"Teambuilding imposes costs, so budget is very important in organizing a program and sticking to the budget"

- Purpose of the teambuilding program

"The program should contain different activities depending on the purpose."

"We have organised programs both for recreation and to change the way of working in teams ..."

"Most often we organized programs for team development ... better communication, better collaboration ..."

"From the documentation I have done I know that the purpose of a program can vary from recreation to learning, development and/or organizational change."

- Objectives set by management and expectations on individual/group/organization-wide results.

"Management is clearly dictating the targets and expected growth. We don't just align ourselves with them and choose the means, the activities ..."

- Needs analysis carried out at organizational/group/individual level.

"Honestly, it is with the psychologist that the work starts, it is the first thing ... he has to identify what the needs and problems are and only then do we develop the programs ..."

"Expectations, needs, wishes of the beneficiaries influence the teambuilding program ..."

"The teambuilding program is not templateable, it has to be adapted to the needs and characteristics of the group."

- Age and educational attainment of participants—homogeneity versus heterogeneity

"It is clear that the age of the participants matters, as well as the age structure of the team ..."

"Depending on how the average age of the group varies, clearly you have to adapt ... activities, conditions ..."

"The age of the participants determines the choice of outdoor and/or indoor activities ..."

- Team structure according to roles/positions

"The teambuilding program is determined by the fact that participants come from different departments/teams or from the same group ..."

"The presence of the boss may lead to breakdown of free communication within the teambuilding program ..."

- Personality structure of each participant

"Clearly you have to take into account when selecting teambuilding activities also the personality structure of the participants ... depending on how they are structured they are more competitive or not, more organized or not, more withdrawn or more social ..."

"Yes, the different personalities of the participants have to be taken into account, otherwise you may not achieve your goals ..."

3.1.4.3. Effects of teambuilding programs

Focus group participants identified impacts at both the organizational and group level, and at the individual level, as follows:

- Improved organizational atmosphere and working environment

"... we have usually seen after the implementation of a program how people in the team have a warmer, less tense relationship, work better together ..."

"... yes, the quality of working relationships increases, the emotional attachment to colleagues and the team increases, the working atmosphere in the team is much more pleasant ..."

" diffusion of knowledge, ideas and perspectives within the company, employees understand and tolerate each other better ..."

- Increased inter- and intra-departmental and team cohesion

"... one effect that I have clearly seen in the company where I work after participating in teambuilding programs is that people communicate better, the dynamics of relationships within and between teams increases, people clearly work better together when they know each other better ..."

"Teambuilding has allowed us to develop teams and increase collaboration within and between teams. I think when people get to know each other better they start to let go of their egos ..."

"... when you share emotions and emotional states with colleagues, and teambuilding is such an opportunity, you clearly feel more attached, otherwise you work with those people with whom you have shared these things ..."

"After participating in teambuilding employees were more willing to communicate openly and constructively and to collaborate..."

- Reducing distance to power

"... during the teambuilding many employees rediscovered their boss, but the boss also rediscovered his team ..."

"... we have had experiences where managers perceived as very rigid have become extremely sympathetic and popular after participating in teambuilding ..."

"... I believe that the presence of the boss in teambuilding could influence the behavior of team members ... they are more restrained, they do what is convenient ..."

"I really think that the relationship with the direct boss can be significantly improved by teambuilding. Communication becomes faster and more direct ..."

- Reduce the number of conflicts in the organization and resolve conflicts between team members more quickly

"I have noticed that after participating in teambuilding employees in the company are more willing to discuss problems and find solutions more easily when they have divergent views."

"The relationship between colleagues is warmer and in general the relationships between employees are clearly better."

"After teambuilding people are more willing to let go of personal egos, solutions are easier to find ..."

- Increasing attachment to the organization, reducing staff turnover, and improving employer branding in the labor market

"Through teambuilding we manage to integrate new employees into the teams, for new employees it is a very good opportunity to get to know the team, the dynamics of relationships within the team, the customs. Thus, integration and synchronization are faster and the number of departures from the company during the integration period is much lower ..."

"Attachment to the company and to the team increases, attachment to the company values increases, this is how we ensure that we decrease departures from the company."

- Increased collaboration and communication between team members

"... one effect that I have clearly seen in the company where I work after participating in teambuilding programs is that people communicate better, the dynamics of relationships within and between teams increases, people clearly work better together when they know each other better ..."

"Teambuilding has allowed us to develop teams and increase collaboration within and between teams. I think when people get to know each other better they start to let go of their egos ..."

"... when you share emotions and emotional states with colleagues, and teambuilding is such an opportunity, you clearly feel more attached, otherwise you work with those people with whom you have shared these things ..."

"After participating in teambuilding employees were more willing to communicate openly and constructively and to collaborate ..."

- Aligning departments within the organization to common goals. Alignment of team members to a common goal/target, pace of work (synchronization of their work)

"Teambuilding helps to better and faster align the team to common goals, common values ..."

"In the company where I work we have succeeded through teambuilding programs to make the communication of future goals easier and thus an easier alignment of the team to these goals"

"Teambuilding has helped us to improve the way we work together, the alignment of team members to common goals and increased the degree of exchange of ideas, knowledge ..."

"Teambuilding helps to align team members to the same pace of work ..."

- Identify/Validate/Reassign roles within the team. Identify new skills of team members

"We used teambuilding when we did an organizational chart redesign and defined new roles. We also used teambuilding to communicate and validate new roles."

"Through teambuilding we discovered new skills of team members that were beneficial and fruitful at team level."

- Better and faster results

"Definitely in the end we are talking about better results, better synchronization of team members which, yes, leads to better results."

"In the company I run the results are visible ... we work better ..."

- When it comes to individual effects, both managers and especially psychologists have identified the following: self-discovery, leadership, work motivation, overcoming personal limits, developing social skills, and regulatory skills.

"Employees have the opportunity to test new skills, to discover a more creative side ..."

"Yes, everyone discovers and self-discovers ..."

"In teambuilding we have the opportunity to identify different patterns: the team creative, the initiative-taker, the industrious, the lazy and the leader ..."

"The psychological component of the group is very important, teambuilding helps you to better understand this component ..."

"In general teambuilding puts the employee in a position to practice his regulatory skills—to communicate, test his will, exercise his attention and share emotions with other colleagues ..."

"Sharing moods and emotions with colleagues develops closer relationships and attachment to the team ..."

"Basically, teambuilding is an opportunity for each employee to better understand if he or she finds himself or herself in the group, in the values of the company ... may be a context in which the employee finds that he or she does not find himself or herself in the values, in the group, cannot synchronize, align ..."

"Clearly it is a context to meet, to socialise, to see how colleagues react in certain situations ..." "I've seen colleagues who have gone beyond some of their limits after participating in teambuilding programs ..."

"we are social beings ... we need to socialise ... during teambuilding colleagues have the opportunity to make friends ..."

3.1.4.4. Measure/evaluate the impact of teambuilding programs

- When it comes to evaluating the effects of teambuilding programs, participants, both managers and psychologists, tend to appreciate that these are seen over time and that program implementation requires consistency to produce results (see Figure 3.1)

"The effects of teambuilding are seen over time, in the long term."

"Results need to be evaluated over time …"

"Teambuilding requires consistency to generate effects …"

"I believe that the effects of teambuilding should be measured at the earliest 6 months after the program …"

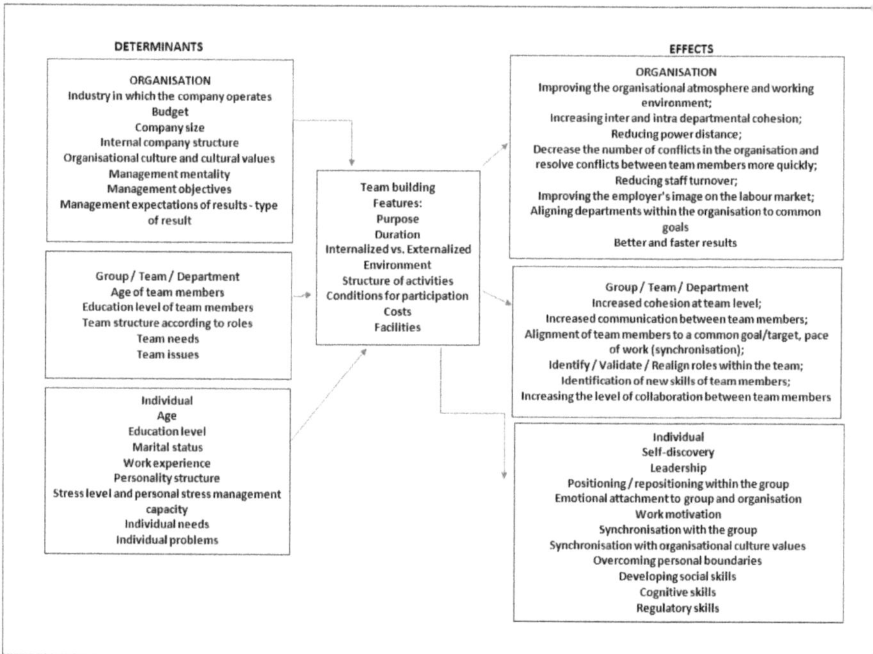

Figure 3.1. Determinants and effects of teambuilding programs.

"I have participated in teambuilding where, at the end, a psychologist, made the participants talk openly about the experience … so, an evaluation can also be done at the end of the program …"

3.2. Measurement of the importance of the determinants and effects of teambuilding programs and identification of their variability according to the size of the company and the level at which it operates—national versus international. Identify the characteristics of an ideal teambuilding programs

3.2.1. Research methods

The quantitative research aimed to measure the degree of importance of the determined factors of teambuilding programs and to correlate these factors with the effects, which is to identify the characteristics of an ideal teambuilding program in relation to the size of the company and the geographical area of the company's operations—national versus international. The quantitative research was conducted from the employers' perspective, that is the sample consisted of managers/specialists/HR directors, being considered the positions with the most expertise in evaluating teambuilding programs, both from the perspective of the determinants and from the perspective of the measured/observed post-implementation effects. For the construction of the sample, the University's social partners—Arges Chamber of Commerce, Industry and Agriculture and Arges Businessmen Association—were trained. Thus, an attempt was made to include in the sample both smaller national/local companies and international/multinational companies, thus ensuring a diversity of experiences and opinions. The data collection instrument was constructed from the focus group results, using five and seven step Likert scales. The questionnaire was sent to 146 companies, and 97 responses were received, with a response rate of approximately 66%. The resulting structure of the sample according to company size is reflected in Table 3.1. The resulting structure of the sample in terms of the level of operation is also shown in Table 3.2.

Table 3.1. Sample structure by company size

Company size	Frequency	Percent
Small	11	11.3
Medium	34	35.1
Big	52	53.6
Total	97	100.0

Table 3.2. Sample structure by level of operation—national vs. international

Level of operations	Frequency	Percent
National	42	43.3
International	55	56.7
Total	97	100.0

3.2.2. Results and discussions

According to the survey results, the majority of HR professionals indicate that the purpose of teambuilding programs should be developmental (58.8%) and recreational (35.1%). Only a minority of participants believe that teambuilding programs should be implemented to support organizational change or organizational learning.

When it comes to the usefulness of teambuilding programs, the central trend across the sample shows that HR staff highly value the effectiveness of such programs at the organizational level (*M*=6.42). However, when it comes to how clear and measurable the effects of teambuilding programs are, the sample mean drops (*M*=5.67); however, this value suggests that in general HR professionals consider the effects of teambuilding programs to be measurable and visible at the organizational level.

Table 3.3. Descriptive statistics—the utility and measurability of teambuilding effects

		The utility of the teambuiding	The outcomes of the teambuilding
N	Valid	97	97
	Missing	0	0
Mean		6.4227	5.6701
Std. Deviation		0.93358	1.34414

3.2.2.1. What are the organizational factors that shape a teambuiding programs? What matters?

According to the research results, management's mindset regarding the organization and implementation of the teambuilding program is the most important determining factor (*M*=6.62), followed by management's objectives (*M*=6.46) and company values (*M*=6.35). At the opposite pole, company size seems to be the least important factor in shaping teambuilding programs. No significant variations were found between national and international companies when it comes to the hierarchy of determining factors of teambuilding programs, although HR specialists in national companies consider management mentality a determining factor of teambuilding programs to a greater extent than specialists in international companies (Table 3.4). The correlation of the determinants of teambuilding programs with company size shows some variability in the results (Table 3.5). Thus, in small companies, the hierarchy is as follows: (1) management mindset, (2) management objectives, and (3) company values. In medium-sized companies, this hierarchy is modified as follows: (1) management mentality, (2) management objectives, and (3) management expected results. Last but not least, in large companies' management mindset and company values occupy the first two positions, while management objectives occupy the third position. Thus, according to the research results, company size is a factor that leads to some variability in perceptions of the antecedents of teambuilding programs.

Table 3.4. Variability of the determinants of teambuilding programs according to the level at which the company operates—national versus international

Level of operations	The industry	The company budget	Company size	The company values	The management mindset	The management objectives	The management expected outcomes
National	5.8293	6.1463	5.4634	6.3902	6.8537	6.5366	6.2439
International	5.9091	6.0909	6.0182	6.3091	6.4545	6.4000	6.2182
Total	5.8750	6.1146	5.7812	6.3437	6.6250	6.4583	6.2292

Table 3.5. Variability of the determinants of teambuilding programs according to company size

Company size	The industry	The company budget	Company size	The company values	The management mindset	The management objectives	The management expected outcomes
Small	5.7000	6.1000	5.2000	6.3000	6.9000	6.5000	5.8000
Medium	5.4118	6.1471	5.6176	6.2941	6.7941	6.5882	6.3529
Big	6.2115	6.0962	6.0000	6.3846	6.4615	6.3654	6.2308
Total	5.8750	6.1146	5.7812	6.3437	6.6250	6.4583	6.2292

3.2.2.2. What are the individual and team factors that shape teambuilding programs? What matters?

According to the research results, the main individual (employee) factors that shape teambuilding programs are the employee's needs (*M*=5.54), the employee's role in the team and organization (*M*=5.39), and the employee's personality (*M*=5.29). Analysis according to the level at which the company operates—national versus international—shows that there is a slight difference in perception regarding the hierarchy of individual factors. While specialists in international companies put the needs of the employee first, specialists in national companies put the role of the employee in the team/organization first. Significant differences in perception were also identified regarding the importance of participant characteristics—age, education, marital status, work experience—in shaping teambuilding programs, in that international companies place a higher importance on these aspects in designing programs compared to national companies.

On the other hand, both international companies and national companies attach higher importance to team (group) factors in shaping teambuilding programs compared to individual (employee) factors. This is supported by the central trends showing that team needs and team problems are the most important aspects evaluated (Tables 3.6 and 3.7).

Table 3.6. Variability of individual and group-determined factors of teambuilding programs according to the level of operation of the company—national versus international

Level of operations	The participants age	The participants education	The participants marital status	The participants professional experience	The team issues	The individual issues
National	4.4286	4.1905	3.0714	4.3095	5.5952	4.7143
International	5.3273	4.9818	4.1455	5.1091	5.7636	5.2182
Total	4.9381	4.6392	3.6804	4.7629	5.6907	5.0000

Analysis of variations by company size shows that in small companies, the personality of the participants is considered the most important individual determinant of teambuilding programs, while in medium and large companies, individual needs are the most important factor (Tables 3.8 and 3.9).

Table 3.7. Variability of individual and group-determined factors of teambuilding programs according to the level of operation of the company—national versus international

Level of operations	The team needs	The individual needs	The hierarchical level of each participant	The personality structure of each participant	The role of each participant
National	6.0476	5.2857	4.0000	5.2143	5.3810
International	6.1455	5.7455	5.0727	5.3636	5.4000
Total	6.1031	5.5464	4.6082	5.2990	5.3918

Table 3.8. Variability of individual and group-determined factors of teambuilding programs by company size

Company size	The participants age	The participants education	The participants marital status	the participant's professional experience	The team issues	The individual issues
Small	5.2727	4.7273	3.7273	4.9091	5.9091	4.9091
Medium	4.8235	4.4118	3.5882	4.7941	6.1176	5.4118
Big	4.9423	4.7692	3.7308	4.7115	5.3654	4.7500
Total	4.9381	4.6392	3.6804	4.7629	5.6907	5.0000

Table 3.9. Variability of individual and group-determined factors of teambuilding programs by company size

Company size	The team needs	The individual needs	The hierarchical level of each participant	The personality structure of each participant	The role of each participant
Small	6.4545	5.2727	4.0909	5.5455	5.0909
Medium	6.2941	5.6765	4.4706	5.2059	5.3824
Big	5.9038	5.5192	4.8077	5.3077	5.4615
Total	6.1031	5.5464	4.6082	5.2990	5.3918

3.2.2.3. Concretely, what are the features of a teambuilding program?

When it comes to the characteristics of a teambuilding programs, the majority of research participants believe that it should be voluntary and that employees should be free to decide whether or not they want to take part in such a program (78.4%). A significant majority of HR specialists (83.5%) believe that teambuilding should be exclusively for employees, not for their family members, who are considered disruptive factors for the successful implementation of the program.

Regarding the optimal duration of a teambuilding program, 78.4% of the participants considered that in order to be effective, a teambuilding program should last at least 2–3 days and take place on weekends (55.7%) and be a mix of indoor and outdoor activities. A significant majority (92.8%) consider that it is up to the company to bear the full cost of the program. When it comes to standards of accommodation services, the majority of participants opted for standards (56.7%).

In Figure 3.2, we have summarized the main characteristics of teambuilding highlighted in our research.

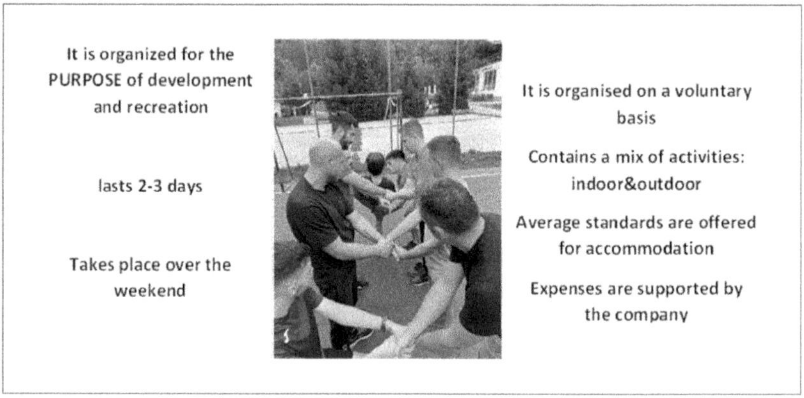

Figure 3.2. The features of a teambuilding program.

3.2.2.4. What are the effects of teambuilding programs at the organizational level?

The analysis of the results shows that all the effects on the organization included in the evaluation were observed within the companies included in the sample, all effects obtaining averages above the value of 5. According to the research results, the four most important benefits of teambuilding programs are: (1) improving the atmosphere at workplace and within the organization (M=6.57), (2) improving communication between team members (M=6.56), (3) increasing cohesion within teams (M=6.55), respectively, and (4) reducing communication barriers between management and executive (M=6.32). On the contrary, the participants believe that teambuilding programs have a smaller positive effect on staff turnover (*M*=5.46) and on the image of the employer on the labor market (*M*=5.70).

Table 3.10. Variability of the effects of teambuilding programs depending on the level of operation of the company—national versus international

Level of operations	Improving the atmosphere within the company—company level	Increasing team cohesion—team level	Better communication between team members—team level	Reducing manager-subordinate communication barriers—company level	Decrease conflicts within the company—company level	Faster resolution of team conflicts—team level
National	6.4286	6.3810	6.3333	6.0238	5.8571	5.7857
International	6.6909	6.6909	6.7455	6.5636	6.1818	6.2727
Total	6.5773	6.5567	6.5670	6.3299	6.0412	6.0619

Comparatively analyzing the results at the level of the two subsamples—national companies versus international companies—a slight difference is observed regarding the hierarchy of the main effects (Tables 3.10 and 3.11). For example, HR specialists from international companies appreciate that the most important result of implementing teambuilding programs is the improvement of communication at the team level, while specialists from national companies put the improvement of the organizational atmosphere first. On the opposite pole, HR specialists from international companies appreciate that the effect observed to a lesser extent is the reduction of staff turnover, while HR specialists from national companies appreciate that the positioning of the employer tree on the labor market is a weaker effect of the programs of teambuilding.

Table 3.11. Variability of the effects of teambuilding programs depending on the level of operation of the company—national versus international

Level of operations	Reducing staff turnover—company level	Strengthening the employer brand image—company level	Aligning departments to common objectives—company level	Aligning team members to common goals—team level	Better outcomes—company level	Faster outcomes—company level	Identifying new individual skills beneficial to the team—team level
National	5.3810	5.2143	5.8095	5.7857	5.8333	5.6190	5.8095
International	5.5273	6.0727	6.2727	6.4364	6.2727	6.1636	6.2727
Total	5.4639	5.7010	6.0722	6.1546	6.0825	5.9278	6.0722

The evaluation of the effects at the employee level (Likert with five steps) shows the fact that all the evaluated aspects were observed by the HR specialists following the implementation of the teambuilding programs. The first three effects at the individual level are: (1) employees became more motivated, (2) employees changed their attitude towards the team/teammates, and (3) employees became more attached to the team and discovered their new skills/qualities.

Table 3.12. Variability of the effects of teambuilding programs depending on individual level—national versus international

Level of operations	Employees have discovered new skills—individual level	Employees have changed their attitude towards the team—individual level	Increasing attachment to colleagues in the team—individual level	Employees became more motivated in carrying out activities—individual level	Employees overstepped their own boundaries—individual level
National	4.2143	4.0952	4.1429	4.1190	3.9048
International	4.2727	4.3818	4.3273	4.4909	4.3818
Total	4.2474	4.2577	4.2474	4.3299	4.1753

3.2.2.5. When and how should the effects/results of teambuilding programs be evaluated?

According to the results of the research, most research participants appreciated that the evaluation of the effects/results of teambuilding programs should be carried out 3 month after the completion of the program (37.1%), respectively 6 month after its completion (34%). Only 27.8% of the participants appreciated that the evaluation should be done right at the end of the teambuilding program. When it comes to evaluation tools, the HR specialists specified evaluation tools such as: structured questionnaire, observation sheet, individual interview, evaluation of predetermined performance indicators at individual or team level, word association tests, etc, measuring individual and team productivity.

3.3. Conclusions

The present study aimed to identify and measure the degree of importance of the determinants (antecedents) of teambuilding programs, as well as the effects on the organization, the team, and the employee.

In general, both human resources specialists and managers, respectively, psychologists see teambuilding programs as a management tool with wide application—regardless of the industry, regardless of the size of the company, regardless of the level at which the company operates (national vs. international). However, this tool is significantly shaped from the perspective of the application of many organizational characteristics, it is not a standardizable tool. Research results show that this tool is used for team and individual development, for organizational culture development/change, and for team/department/employee alignment to common goals/objectives. Also, teambuilding is considered an informal or semi-formal organizational context in which the conditions are created for discovery and self-discovery, for building the individual/group/organizational mentality, for sharing some emotions and feelings that are not expressed in formal work contexts, organizational freedom and stress relief, building and strengthening bonds and relationships, developing synergy and attachment.

The most important objectives that were the basis of the design and implementation of teambuilding programs are: the implementation of organizational change programs; organizational chart redesign, validation of new roles, redefinition of roles; aligning teams/departments to objectives, common goals; uniting teams, increasing cohesion, improving communication; increasing performance at the organization level, increasing performance at the team level; increasing attachment to the organization.

In the design of teambuilding programs, the psychologist—the specialist in organizational psychology—should be the first involved to identify the needs and problems of the group and the individual. Quantitative research reveals that team needs and problems are the most important factors that should shape teambuilding programs.

Also, the results of the quantitative research reveal the fact that the characteristics of the employees participating in the teambuilding programs—age, education, marital status, professional experience—are considered in the design of the teambuilding programs. In international companies, a higher importance is given to these aspects in the design of programs compared to national companies.

When it comes to the organizational factors that shape teambuilding programs, management mindset appears to be the most important factor, regardless of the size of the company or the level at which it operates. Interestingly,

HR managers believe that using this tool is more a matter of mindset than of resources. Added to this factor are the objectives pursued by management and the values of the organizational culture. Therefore, the use of teambuilding programs as a management tool is directly related to management thinking and organizational culture. On the other hand, teambuilding is a tool for developing organizational culture. Thus, the relationship between teambuilding and organizational culture is a complex one.

The usefulness of teambuilding programs is widely recognized, although from the perspective of measuring the effects, there are also points of view that they are sometimes more difficult to measure. At the organizational level, the most important benefits are related to the improvement of the working atmosphere within the organizational/team framework, the increase of team cohesion, and the improvement of vertical and horizontal communication. The research reveals that teambuilding contributes to a lesser extent to the reduction of staff turnover and the formation of the image of the employer brand on the labor market.

When it comes to the employee, the most important benefits of participating in teambuilding programs are: increased motivation, change in attitude towards colleagues and towards the team, and increased attachment to those with whom they work and collaborate on a regular basis. Also, the employee often discovers, in this context, new skills, new qualities, and new perspectives. Sometimes these contexts validate or not the fit of the employee in the team, the ability to synchronize with the team.

Research participants also identified a number of factors that moderate the effects of teambuilding programs. For example, the presence of the direct boss can sometimes lead to the cancellation of organizational freedom and formalism, which leads to carefully considered behaviors on the part of participating employees. On the other hand, the presence of family members in teambuilding programs is considered a disturbing factor that negatively influences the achievement of the effects and the achievement of the objectives of teambuilding programs. Last but not least, the mandatory participation seems to diminish the effects of teambuilding programs.

Although the research clearly reveals the fact that teambuilding is a managerial tool that cannot be standardized, being adapted to the particularities of each use and company, according to the research results, several organizational characteristics of an ideal teambuilding program were identified. Thus, a teambuilding program must be built on a voluntary basis, with employees having the freedom to decide whether or not they want to take part in such a program. Only company employees participate in the program, regardless of whether they come from a single department or from several departments. The teambuilding program should be organized on the weekend, to introduce a relaxed atmosphere and a sense of organizational freedom, it should last no more than 2–3 days. Within the program there should be a mix of activities subordinated to the purpose of development and/or recreation, organized both indoors and outdoors. The company should cover all costs and provide participants with average accommodation standards.

When it comes to evaluating the effects of teambuilding programs, research participants seem to be aligned with the idea that results appear over time and that evaluation should be done 3–6 months after the completion of the program, although they acknowledge that a first evaluation can be carried out even at the completion of the program but this would only measure the mood of the group/individual, without a real assessment of the benefits of participation. Also, the participants recognize that the psychologist's

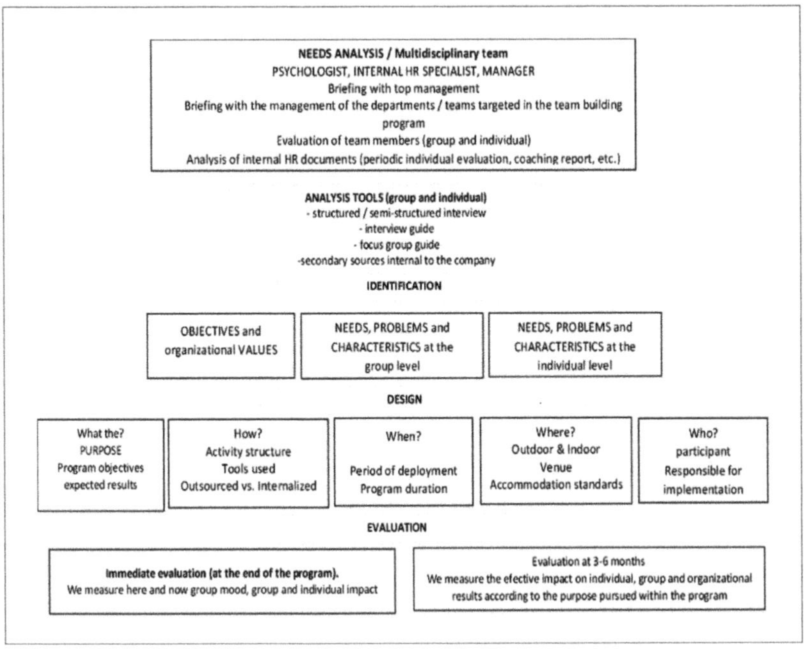

Figure 3.3. The stages of designing and evaluating the results of teambuilding programs.

involvement in this stage is important, as he is part of a team—manager, HR specialist, psychologist. The tools proposed for evaluation are various—structured questionnaires, interview guide, observation sheet, measurable performance indicators sheet, etc.

All stages of designing and evaluating the results of teambuilding programs highlighted by our research are summarized in Figure 3.3.

Bibliography

Allameh, S. M., & Abbas, S. K. (2010). The Relationship between Knowledge Management Practices and Innovation Level in Organizations: Case Study of Sub-companies of Selected Corporations in the City of Esfahan. *Journal of Business Case Studies (JBCS)*, *6*(1).

Bărculescu, C., & Bâgu, C. (2001). Managementul producţiei, vol. II—Politici manageriale de producţie.

Berson, Y., Nemanich, L. A., Waldman, D. A., Galvin, B. M., & Keller, R. T. (2006). Leadership and Organizational Learning: A Multiple Levels Perspective. *The Leadership Quarterly*, *17*(6), 577–94.

Chen, S. C., & Quester, P. G. (2006). Modeling Store Loyalty: Perceived Value in Market Orientation Practice. *Journal of Services Marketing*, *20*(3), 188–98.

Cristina, M. O. R. A. (2008). Leadership şi dezvoltare organizaţională în administraţia publică locală din România. *Revista Transilvană de Ştiinţe Administrative*, *10*(21), 29–46

Dimas, I. D., Torres, P., Rebelo, T., & Lourenço, P. R. (2023). Paths to Team Success: A Configurational Analysis of Team Effectiveness. *Human Performance*, 1–25.

Dong, B. (2023). A Systematic Review of the Organizational Inertia Literature and Future Outlook. *International Journal of Education and Humanities*, *8*(2), 119–23.

Emadzade, M. K., Mashayekhi, B., & Abdar, E. (2012). Knowledge Management Capabilities and Organizational Performance. *Interdisciplinary Journal of Contemporary Research in Business*, *3*(11), 781–90.

Hassan, S., & Al-Hakim, L. A. Y. (2011). The Relationships among Critical Success Factors of Knowledge Management, Innovation and

Organizational Performance: A Conceptual Framework. In *2011 International Conference on Management and Artificial Intelligence* (pp. 94–103).

Hillman, A. J., & Keim, G. D. (2001). Shareholder Value, Stakeholder Management, and Social Issues: What's the Bottom Line? *Strategic Management Journal*, *22*(2), 125–39.

Ho, L. A. (2008). What Affects Organizational Performance? The Linking of Learning and Knowledge Management. *Industrial Management & Data Systems*, *108*(9), 1234–54.

Kaplan, R. S., & Norton, D. P. (1992). *Measures that Drive Performance*. Harvard Business Review.

Kurtipek, S., & Güngör, N. (2019). Individual Innovation: A Research on Sports Manager Candidates. *Journal of Education and Learning*.

Lau, C. M., & Ngo, H. Y. (2004). The HR System, Organizational Culture, and Product Innovation. *International Business Review*, *13*(6), 685–703.

Law, K. S., & Wong, C. S. (1999). Multidimensional Constructs M Structural Equation Analysis: An Illustration Using the Job Perception and Job Satisfaction Constructs. *Journal of Management*, *25*(2), 143–60.

Mahapatro, B. B. (2022). *Human Resource Management*. PG Department of Business Management.

Nawab, S., Nazir, T., Zahid, M. M., & Fawad, S. M. (2015). Knowledge Management, Innovation and Organizational Performance. *International Journal of Knowledge Engineering*, *1*(1), 43–8

Noruzy, A., Dalfard, V. M., Azhdari, B., Nazari-Shirkouhi, S., & Rezazadeh, A. (2013). Relations between Transformational Leadership, Organizational Learning, Knowledge Management, Organizational Innovation, and Organizational Performance: An Empirical Investigation of Manufacturing Firms. *The International Journal of Advanced Manufacturing Technology*, *64*, 1073–85.

Orlitzky, M. (2008). Corporate Social Performance and Financial Performance: A Research Synthesis. In Andrew Crane et al. (eds), *The Oxford Handbook of Corporate Social Responsibility*, Oxford Academic.

Saeidi, S. P., Sofian, S., Saeidi, P., Saeidi, S. P., & Saaeidi, S. A. (2015). How Does Corporate Social Responsibility Contribute to Firm Financial Performance? The Mediating Role of Competitive Advantage,

Reputation, and Customer Satisfaction. *Journal of Business Research, 68*(2), 341–50.

Seaver, D. S. (2000). Effect of Transformational Leadership in a Cross-Cultural Organization: A Case Study. Capella University.

Senge, P. M. (2006). *The Fifth Discipline: The Art and Practice of the Learning Organization*. Broadway Business.

Singh, S. K., Gupta, S., Busso, D., & Kamboj, S. (2021). Top Management Knowledge Value, Knowledge Sharing Practices, Open Innovation and Organizational Performance. *Journal of Business Research 128*, 788–98.

Snow, C. C., & Hrebiniak, L. G. (1980). Strategy, Distinctive Competence, and Organizational Performance. *Administrative Science Quarterly*, 317–36.

Spear, S. J. (2009). *High-Velocity Edge: How Market Leaders Leverage Operational Excellence to Beat the Competition*. McGraw-Hill Education.

Templeton, G. F., Lewis, B. R., & Snyder, C. A. (2002). Development of a measure for the organizational learning construct. *Journal of Management Information Systems 19*(2), 175–218.

Valmohammadi, C. (2010). Identification and Prioritization of Critical Success Factors of Knowledge Management in Iranian SMEs: An Experts' View. *African Journal of Business Management 4*(6), 915–24.

CHAPTER 4

Warm-Up and Knowledge Activities

Daniel Roşu, Sebastian Enache, Valentina Ştefănică, and Florin Cojanu

Summary: Warm-up and familiarization activities help create a positive atmosphere and build a solid foundation for further collaboration in teambuilding activities. They are designed to create a comfortable environment and facilitate interaction between team members (Alecu, 2021).

These activities are performed in the form of warm-up games, to get to know each other, to lay the foundations for informal activities, to "break the initial communication barriers" and to increase the level of psychological comfort between the participants. The following distinct categories of activities stand out in this chapter: *Energizing games, physical stretching activities, and icebreakers.*

Energizing games are useful for keeping participants' energy and engagement high, being an effective tool to revitalize and sustain an interactive and dynamic environment during meetings or group events. Stretching exercises—These have the role of preparing the body for the following physical activities, reducing the risk of injuries, and improving the flexibility and mobility of the participants. Icebreakers are ideal for motivating everyone at the start of a meeting or introducing newcomers (Badau, 2018).

At this stage, elements of human touch between group members can be introduced. The human touch can be a valuable component in teambuilding activities, helping to build relationships, improve communication, and strengthen team spirit, but it must be used with sensitivity and respect for individual preferences and boundaries.

Keywords: Warm-up, short exercises, question and answer sessions

4.1. The role and content of warm-up and familiarization exercises

Warm-up and familiarization activities in a teambuilding event are meant to help participants feel comfortable in each other's presence and form initial bonds. These activities are designed to encourage communication, collaboration, and trust building between team members (Stefanica, 2018).

Warming up in teambuilding activities is an essential element to prepare the participants for the upcoming activities. The role of warming up in a teambuilding context is similar to that in sports activities or physical and mental training. It includes several aspects (Rosu, 2022):

- Creating a positive and open atmosphere: A well-done warm-up can improve the mood of participants and create a more pleasant atmosphere conducive to collaboration and engagement. On the other hand, warm-up exercises can help reduce stress and anxiety, allowing participants to feel more relaxed and open to future team activities (Rosu et al., 2022).

- Physical and mental preparation: Light physical exercises or breathing techniques can help warm-up the muscles and prepare the body for the intense or interactive activities ahead. On the other hand, a proper warm-up can improve participants' focus and attention, mentally preparing them for tasks or exercises that require active involvement and concentration.
- Facilitate interaction and collaboration: Warm-up exercises can be designed to help participants get to know each other better, interact, and start working together in a more open way. Also, a good start to teambuilding activities can strengthen team relations and stimulate collaboration, trust, and communication between participants.

Among the recommendations for the appropriate choice of warm-up and familiarization activities, we can prioritize the use of the following types of games and activities:

- *Energizing games:* These games are designed to raise the energy level of the participants and get them moving. They can involve short physical activities and bring a positive attitude to the group.
- *Stretching activities,* such as stretching exercises.
- *Icebreakers or pre-acquaintance games*—these are fun and easy activities that aim to help participants get to know each other better. These can involve interesting questions, group activities, or even word games.

Within the knowledge activities, the ones indicated for the beginning are the presentation games. These may involve each participant presenting their name, professional experience, and a personal passion. This helps team members learn more about each other.

Question and Answer (Q&A) sessions can be just as useful: Participants can have the opportunity to ask their peers or the facilitator questions about their area of expertise or their experiences.

The purpose of these activities is to facilitate bonding between team members, build trust, and pave the way for more effective collaboration within the teambuilding event and subsequently in day-to-day work activities (Rosu, 2008).

It is important that these activities are well planned and have a balance between fun and their main purpose, which is to develop a sense of community and collaboration among team members.

Introductory activities can introduce elements of human touch between group members. The human touch in teambuilding activities can play an important role in facilitating communication, building relationships, and building trust in a team. While not required in all team building scenarios, the human touch can bring multiple benefits (Permann-Graham et al., 2022):

- Promoting emotional and social connection: When participants touch or interact physically, this can help build a relationship of trust and comfort between team members; The human touch can help create a sense of team unity and cohesion as members begin to feel more connected and closer.
- Improving communication and collaboration: Human touch can facilitate deeper understanding and help non-verbal communication between participants, which can be helpful in effective collaboration. In certain teambuilding activities that require touch or physical interaction, participants are encouraged to work together, which can strengthen team spirit.
- Building a positive atmosphere: The human touch can help create a more relaxed and open atmosphere in teambuilding activities, making it easier for participants to feel comfortable and actively engage.

However, introducing elements of human touch between members of a work group has some limits and considerations. Thus, it is important to consider the comfort and personal limits of each participant. Some people may be more reserved about physical touch or have certain sensitivities, and this should be respected. It is also essential to consider the cultural context and social norms. What may be acceptable in one culture may not be as well received in another! (Catanescu, 2019).

4.2. Examples of energizing games

Energizer games are short and interactive activities or exercises carried out within a teambuilding to increase the energy level and revitalize the participants. The main purpose of these games is to raise the level of engagement and refresh the attention and enthusiasm of the group members.

These energizing activities are designed to counteract the fatigue or monotony that can occur during a long meeting or intense work session. They can be used to change the pace, stimulate interaction, and build team spirit in a fun and dynamic way (Stanescu et al., 2004).

Energizing game features include:

- *Short and interactive:* These activities usually don't last long—they are meant to be short and focused to revitalize participants in a short amount of time.
- *Physical or mental:* Energizing games can involve physical movement, such as dancing, short exercises, or group games, or they can be more geared toward mental activities, such as riddles, quizzes, or quick-thinking games.
- *Designed to create a positive atmosphere:* These are designed to bring a smile to the faces of the participants and to encourage a positive attitude in the group.
- Flexible and adaptable: Energizing games can be adapted to the size of the group, the available space, and the specific objectives of the meeting or event.

Examples of energizing games include warm-up games, rhythmic group movements, quick question and answer games, cooperative activities, or exercises that require active participation and involvement of the whole group.

Activity 1: Circle dance

Participants form a circle and follow simple dance moves at a brisk pace for several minutes. This activity can be accompanied by music and can be a great way to start a teambuilding session.

Activity 2: Breathing exercises

Leading the group through simple breathing exercises can help with relaxation and focus. For example, deep breathing exercises or relaxation techniques can help participants feel calmer and improve their mood.

Activity 3: Fast movement games

Activities such as "Senses Alert" require participants to react quickly to certain commands or changes in direction. This can be done by running short, jumping, lifting the knees, etc.

Activity 4: Balloon in the air

Activities involving a ball or balloon can be energizing and fun. For example, a quick ball/balloon toss and catch game between participants can be an interactive and dynamic way to keep the group energized.

Rules of conduct: Participants are divided into groups of 4–6 members, each group receiving a balloon to inflate. The members of the groups hold hands and form a circle, trying to keep the balloon in the air or transport it to a certain place by hitting it, without releasing their hands.

Activity 5: Touch the Box

"Touch the box" is a team game that involves touching an object with a certain part of the body. The box can be replaced with a large beach ball or a plastic bottle.

Rules of conduct: The players sit around the object, which is placed on the ground. The aim of the game is for all players to touch the object at the same time with a certain part of the body, such as a finger, toe, knee, elbow, shoulder, etc. Then, the object transport is required: Players must transport the object using only the previously indicated body extremities to a pre-indicated place that is 4–6 m away. If the object falls, players must start over.

Activity 6: "Follow the Leader": Dance

One of the participants is designated as the leader, and all the others must follow him, repeating the movements he makes. Each person in the group will have the opportunity to be a leader, thus creating an atmosphere of joy and involvement.

These energizing games are meant to be fun and bring a positive note to the group, helping to change the pace and tone to prepare participants for the next teambuilding activities.

Activity 7: Human Nodes

At the end of the warm-up and familiarization activities, this game can be successfully used to facilitate physical contact between people. The human touch can be a valuable component in teambuilding activities, helping to build relationships, improve communication, and strengthen team spirit, but it must be used with sensitivity and respect for individual preferences and boundaries. Poses of this application can be seen in Figure 4.1.

Figure 4.1. Human nodes.

Rules of conduct: Form a large circle with 7–8 participants. The requirement is for everyone to reach out in a circle and hold the hand of someone else in the circle. With their hands crossed, each person in the circle must hold the left hand of another person in the circle (who is not directly next to them) and the right hand of another person (who is not adjacent). The objective is to create a "new human" without the hands being free or coming apart. Participants must communicate and collaborate to find a solution to break free without breaking the chain of hands. They must find ways to move, go under or over the hands of others, and rearrange positions to free the human knot. The goal is for the group to work together to solve the "new human" and reach a position where all participants are connected in a continuous circle, but no longer entangled.

Benefits of this exercise: Encourages participants to communicate clearly and openly. Without communication, resolution becomes more difficult. It also encourages thinking beyond traditional methods to solve the problem. Sometimes, unconventional solutions are the key. Emphasizes the importance of teamwork and highlights that success depends on the effort and contribution of each team member.

Activity 8. The snake catches its tail

Rules of conduct: Participants form a circle and hold hands together so that everyone is connected and creates a closed circle. The circle opens so that at one end is the person who designates the "snake's head" and at the other end is the person who designates the "snake's tail." The purpose of the "snake head" is to catch its own tail without breaking the hand chain. Participants must collaborate and communicate with each other to adjust their movements and positions so that the "snake's head" ends up catching the tail while keeping the chain of hands intact (see Figure 4.2).

Benefits of this exercise: The app promotes strategic thinking and finding the best ways to approach problem solving without breaking the chain of hands. Finding the balance between quick movements and attention to maintaining the chain of hands can be the key to success.

4.3. Examples of stretching exercises

Stretching exercises are an important part of the teambuilding warm-up. Here are some examples of stretching exercises that can be included in warm-up sessions (Stadler-Altmann, 2021):

Figure 4.2. The snake catches its tail.

Activity 1: Stretching the lower limbs

Exercises such as forward bending (bending the trunk forward) can be done to stretch the back and leg muscles. Also, stretching your legs on the floor, alternating between leg flexion and ankle extension, can help relax your calf muscles.

Activity 2: Hip and torso rotation

Hip and trunk rotations can help stretch and relax the muscles in your abdomen and back.

Activity 3: Stretching the shoulders and arms

Lifting and stretching your arms overhead, crossing your arms in front of your chest, and rolling your shoulders can help relax your shoulder and upper back muscles.

Activity 4: Neck exercises

Turning the head slightly to the left and right, bending the head towards the shoulders to stretch the muscles of the neck and back, can be beneficial for relaxation and flexibility.

Activity 5: Back exercises

Stretching the back while standing, by bending the trunk to the side, or by stretching the back muscles through yoga poses, can help prepare the spine for physical activity.

During teambuilding, it is important to include such stretching exercises, giving participants the opportunity to warm-up properly and prepare their bodies for the activities to come, especially when the challenges provided by the facilitators are more demanding, like climbing heights or adventure applications (see Chapter 1). It is advisable that these exercises be done at a moderate pace, respecting the limits of each participant, and incorporating breathing exercises to improve relaxation and mobility (Dario, 2021).

4.4. Examples of icebreaker activities

Icebreaker activities and questions are fun little games that facilitate getting to know each other between new and older colleagues (Stancu, 2018). Knowledge games are essential in teambuilding to help team members get to know each other, get to know their colleagues better, and establish stronger bonds in a fun and interactive way (Badiu, 1995). Here are some examples of knowledge games that you can use in teambuilding:

Activity 1: Name-Adjective-Thing Game

Rules of conduct: Participants introduce themselves using an adjective that starts with the same letter as their name and a favorite thing that starts with the same letter as the first letter of their name. For example, "Simona the Amazing, who loves Skiing."

Activity 2: A great pair

Rules of conduct: Each participant receives a ticket with the name of a colleague from the group (preferably of the opposite gender). The goal of the game is to find your partner and get to know them. Participants must look for the person whose name is on their ticket and talk to them for a few minutes. After all participants have found their pair from the ticket, they must introduce their partner to the group based on the information found.

Benefits of this exercise: In this way, the whole group will have the opportunity to meet someone new and make new friends.

Activity 3: Coins with memories

Rules of conduct: Take a box and fill it with coins inscribed with a year that is not before the birthday of the youngest member of the team. Each team member is asked to take a coin from the box and tell a story, memory, or other significant event that happened to them that year.

Benefits of this exercise: Multiple rounds can be organized in situations where stories are rather short or if team members want to have the opportunity to develop their story to learn more about themselves.

Activity 4: Mood pictures

Rules of conduct: Several images are used, such as clippings from newspapers, postcards, and posters, images from magazines, or different images from the Internet can be printed. Images should feature landscapes, cities, people, shapes, or animals, with a mix of colors and perspectives. All images must be placed face up, and each team member will choose an image that represents their mood at that moment. After everyone has chosen an image, he is asked to explain why he made the choice, what feelings and experiences the image evokes.

Benefits of this exercise: This activity allows you to set the mood of the group in a creative and original way. It is a great way to start a meeting or workshop. Team members should not always be asked to choose an image that reflects their mood. It can also represent their expectations from a workshop, their impressions of a current project, or what they intend to do at the end of the day.

Activity 5: Mutual interviews

The participants are divided into pairs, and each person interviews their partner to find out interesting things about them, such as hobbies, favorite trips, imaginary superpowers, etc. Then each person introduces their partner to the rest of the group.

Activity 6: Two Lies, One Truth

Rules of conduct: The activity is carried out in groups of about 3–4 people. Each person in the group is asked to think of two true facts and one lie about themselves. The more memorable the facts and the more believable the lies, the more fun the game will be! Then, each team member presents those little stories, and the group says which of the three they think is the lie.

Benefits of this exercise: Information shared this way can be used later to start a conversation and get to know the people working together.

Activity 7: Back-to-back drawings

Rules of conduct: The team is divided into groups of two, and in each group, colleagues will sit back-to-back. The first person is given a pencil and a piece of paper, and the second person is shown a picture of an easy object to draw. The first (the one who sees the picture) has to describe the picture without revealing its name, and the second has to draw the object. The first is allowed to describe the shape, size, texture, and other details, as long as they do not directly tell their partner to draw a flower, for example. After the drawings are finished, they are compared to the originals to see if the verbal instructions were helpful.

Benefits of this exercise: This fun activity helps improve communication and listening skills. It is also an opportunity for teams to be creative, show originality, and think creatively to describe their colleague's image.

Activity 8: The difference game

Rules of conduct: The team is divided into two groups, aligned face-to-face. Team A members have a short observation period (15–30 s) during which they must memorize as many details as possible about the people in front of them. They then return as the members of Team B change as many aspects of their appearance as possible. Almost anything is allowed, and one can, for example, change the order of the participants or change the hairstyle. After 45 s, Team A returns. They then have 5–10 min to find out what has changed. The available time can be adapted to the size of the group.

Benefits of this exercise: The team can thus practice non-verbal communication in a limited time during the appearance change phase.

Activity 9: Map of passions

Rules of conduct: Each participant draws a map of their passions on a sheet of paper or on a board, marking their main activities or interests.

Benefits of this exercise: This can be a great way to discover commonalities between team members.

Activity 10: The common denominator

Rules of conduct: Common denominator is an interactive group game that can be played with many participants. The game encourages making connections between the people in the group and identifying the similarities and differences in the list below. In a predefined time of 10–15 min the participants have to complete 1–2–3 (clearly defined number at the beginning of the application) names that have the characteristics mentioned in the adjacent list. An example of the game can be seen in Figure 4.3.

Figure 4.3. The common denominator.

The application form may include the following elements:

My name is:

………………………………………

Request: Find 3 people each and write their names on your list

I'm looking for someone who:

- Celebrates their birthday in the same month as you
- Reads the press regularly
- Has a brother and a sister

- Knows a lot about the geography of Europe
- First name starts with the same letter as yours
- Likes traditional music
- Likes to prepare food
- Runs regularly in the morning
- Was on vacation at the seaside at least 3 times
- Reads detective fiction
- Goes to the theater at least once a year
- Is fascinated by anticipatory literature
- Visited at least 3 countries in Europe
- Wears the same shoe number as you
- Has ever been a volunteer

Benefits of this exercise: Thanks to this fun game, team members will find things in common that they might not otherwise have had the opportunity to discover. It is also a good way to bring members of a divided team together (Balint, 2009).

Activity 11: Knowledge in motion

Rules of conduct: The participants are divided into two circles, one inside and one outside, which rotate at regular intervals. During the rotation, each person has a limited amount of time to introduce their colleague in front of them or to answer a question given by the facilitator.

Activity 12: Birthday row

Rules of conduct: The entire team is asked to line up by date of birth, without members consulting each other. The use of different forms of communication can be encouraged, such as sign language (possibly of each person's zodiac sign), gestures, or simply pushing. And if you want to put more pressure on team members and spice up the game, you can add a time limit.

Benefits of this exercise: In addition to learning each other's dates of birth, this activity encourages the team to communicate non-verbally to achieve a common goal. Although this exercise can be difficult and even frustrating, it also improves problem formulation and non-verbal communication skills and fosters cooperation.

Activity 13: Knowledge test

Rules of conduct: Make up fun and interesting questions about the team members (for example, what is their favorite food, what are their hobbies, etc.) and then organize a quiz where the participants have to answer these questions. This will help them learn new things about each other. An example of this application can be seen in Figure 4.4.

Figure 4.4. Knowledge test.

Benefits of this exercise: These knowledge games are great for encouraging communication, building trust, and building bonds between team members in an interactive and fun way. They contribute to the atmosphere of cooperation and openness needed within a team to work together more effectively and develop stronger relationships.

Activity 14: Code of conduct

Rules of conduct: On a whiteboard, write two categories titled Important and Pleasant. Then, the group is asked what they think they will need in these categories to successfully participate in that teambuilding. Group members choose ideas that they find both important and enjoyable. These values are noted in a common document to establish the code of conduct for workshops. This list will act as a reminder to the team of the values that must be adhered to.

Benefits of this exercise: This exercise helps the team establish rules and values that everyone agrees on. Establishing group norms and values and holding everyone accountable through a code of conduct creates a sense of cohesion.

Activity 15. Salt and pepper

Rules of conduct: Facilitators will draw up a list of objects from the same family that go together (salt and pepper, left and right socks, day and night, bread and butter, yin and yang, etc.). Write these words on different pieces of paper and stick one piece of paper on the back of each team member. Team members are asked to mingle with others and find out what they wrote on their backs by asking questions that can only be answered with a yes or no (e.g., Am I sweet? Feel good? Am I cold?). After all the participants have discovered who they are, they will have to find the colleague with whom they each match.

Benefits of this exercise: The team can use this game to get to know each other better and improve their communication skills. Within a large team, this exercise allows interaction with colleagues with whom one communicates less in working conditions.

Bibliography

Alecu A., Botila V., & Cojanu F. (2021). Effects of Recreational Activities Nautical Sports in Leisure on the Strengthening of Motor Skills in Children of School Age. *Bulletin of the Transilvania University of Brașov. Series IX: Sciences of Human Kinetics*. <https://doi.org/10.31926/but.shk.2021.14.63.1.15>.

Badau, D., & Badau, A. (2018). The Motric, Educational, Recreational and Satisfaction Impact of Adventure Education Activities in the Urban Tourism Environment. *Sustainability (Switzerland) 10*(6), 1–13. <https://doi.org/10.3390/su10062106>.

Badiu T. (1995). *Exercitii și jocuri de mișcare pentru clasele I–IV*. Galati: Ed Alma.

Balint Gh. (2009). *Jocurile dinamice—o alternativă pentru optimizarea lectiei de educatie fizică cu teme din fotbal în învătământul gimnazial*. Editura PIM Iași.

Catanescu, A. C. (2019). Analyze "Wellness Self-perception" at the Level of Young People for Increasing the Quality of Life. *Bulletin of the Transilvania University of Braşov. Series IX: Sciences of Human Kinetics.* <https://doi.org/10.31926/but.shk.2019.12.61.2.49>.

Dario C., & D'Arando C. (2021). Teaching Styles and Outdoor Education to Promote Non-linear Learning. *Journal of Physical Education and Sport.* <https://doi.org/10.7752/jpes.2021.s1054>

Perrmann-Graham, J., Liu, J., Cangioni, C., & Spataro, S. E. (2022). Fostering Psychological Safety: Using Improvisation as a Team Building Tool in Management Education. *International Journal of Management Education 20*(2), 100617. <https://doi.org/10.1016/j.ijme.2022.100617>.

Rosu, D. (2008). *Animation Techniques Mountain Teambuilding.* Universitaria Craiova Publishing House.

Rosu D. (2022). Effect of Extracurricular Interest of Students in the Field of Physical Education and Sports on the Development of Entrepreneurial Skills. *Journal of Physical Education and Sport.* <https://doi.rg/10.7752/jpes.2022.08244>.

Rosu D., Cojanu F., Stefanica V., Enache S. (2022). Experimental Management of Work Collectives Through Social and Socialization Activities. *Journal of Physical Education and Sport.* <https://doi.org/10.7752/jpes.2022.07218>.

Stadler-Altmann U. (2021). *Indoors and Outdoors: Schoolyards as Learning and Playing Opportunities. Free University of Bolzano, Italy.* <https://doi.org/10.7752/jpes.2021.s1062>.

Stancu, M. (2018). *Improving Interpersonal Relations in Students Using Specific Motric Activities. The European Proceedings of Social & Behavioural Sciences EpSBS.* <https://doi.org/10.15405/epsbs.2019.08.03.2630.0>.

Stefanica, V., & Rosu, D. (2018). Evaluation of the Working Groups in the Group Cohesion Perspective, in the Project Boboc Camp, 2018. *Journal of Physical Education and Sport.* <https://doi.org/10.7752/jpes.2018.s5322>.

Stănescu M., Ciolcă C., & Urzeală, C. (2004). *Jocul de mişcare – metodă şi mijloc de instruire în educatie fizică şi sport.* Ed. Cartea Universitară, Bucureşti.

CHAPTER 5

Trust-Building activities

Daniel Roşu, Valentina Ştefănică, Sebastian Enache, and Florin Cojanu

Summary: Trust-building activities in teambuilding are designed to strengthen relationships between team members and create an environment where they can rely on each other. Key features of these activities include collaboration in informal settings—participants are placed in non-competitive or challenging contexts; trust and vulnerability exercises—involve sharing personal experiences against a background of understanding and empathy between team members and encourages team members to reveal more personal aspects of themselves and build genuine connection; typical interactive games and activities. Developing the opportunity to give and receive constructive feedback is an important element in building trust in the abilities and contributions of each team member.

Keywords: Informal situations, non-competitive contexts, challenging contexts, trust vulnerability, constructive feedback

Trust-building activities are actions and exercises specifically planned to improve relationships and trust between members of a team (Engebø et al., 2022; Turaga, 2013; Hakanen, 2015). Dyer et al. (2013) claims that these activities are aimed at strengthening collaboration, improving communication, and increasing the sense of team unity.

5.1. Trust-building techniques

To create an environment where team members can rely on each other (Tseng & Yeh, 2013; Depping et al., 2016) different techniques can be applied such as:

- Open and clear communication: Team members will be encouraged to communicate freely and share ideas, thoughts, and concerns without fear of judgment or excessive criticism.
- Building trust step-by-step: Planning activities that promote mutual trust between team members are the most direct approaches to this end. Games and exercises that require collaboration and mutual support can strengthen team bonds and trust.
- Clear definition of common goals: Ensuring that all team members understand and share the same goals and values support the cultivation of trust. This can motivate them to work together to achieve the same goals.

- Building personal relationships: Encouraging social interactions between team members outside of the work environment reinforces a trusting work environment. Organizing informal activities or social events such as teambuilding allows colleagues to get to know each other better and develop closer personal relationships.
- Resolving conflicts constructively: When conflicts or tensions arise in the team, it is important to address these issues in a constructive and empathetic way to avoid escalation and maintain a positive work environment.
- Recognition and appreciation of individual contributions: Encouraging public recognition of individual achievements and contributions of each team member can successfully build self-confidence and mutual support within the team.
- Participative leadership and equal involvement: When the team leader is open and involved in activities, but also provides space for the participation and contribution of all team members in decision-making and problem-solving, it contributes essentially to strengthening trust in the organization.

Teambuilding activities are based on providing non-competitive or challenging contexts (Burm et al., 2019; Avalos-Bevan & Bascopé, 2017). Thus, the focus should be on collaboration, encouraging creativity, and strengthening mutual trust within the team. It is important that all activities are geared toward learning and growth, not direct competition between members.

5.2. Conditions for applying trust-building techniques

Introducing and exploring vulnerability in teambuilding activities can help strengthen relationships and develop an atmosphere of trust and openness in the team. Integrating and managing the vulnerability of participants in such a context can be done through:

- Creating a safe space: Activity facilitators will ensure that participants feel comfortable and safe to share feelings, experiences, and thoughts without fear of judgment or criticism. This can be done by setting clear rules and encouraging mutual respect in discussions.

- Carrying out activities that encourage vulnerability: Exercises will be planned that ask participants to share personal stories, talk about their challenges, or expose certain sensitive aspects of their lives. This can help build trust and create a stronger connection between team members.
- Planning empathy exercises: Activities that require contemplating others' perspectives or understanding, or directly feeling the emotions that others are going through, can help develop team empathy and increase trust through mutual understanding.
- Facilitating open discussions: Holding discussion sessions where participants talk freely about their fears, failures, or challenges they face can help normalize vulnerability and understand that it is okay for anyone to be vulnerable in front of teammates.
- Modeling positive behavior: Leaders or facilitators should also show vulnerability to create an environment where participants feel comfortable expressing their own vulnerabilities. This may encourage others to do the same.
- Building trust over time: As participants feel safer and more comfortable in the teambuilding environment, they will be more likely to share and explore vulnerability.
- Encouraging accountability: Helping participants understand that vulnerability is an act of courage, along with understanding the importance of taking responsibility for their own feelings and experiences.

Trust-building teambuilding activities encourage team members to be authentic and connect with their colleagues in an honest and deep way. Such authentic connections (Everhart et al., 2016; Michalec et al., 2021; Robbins, 2018) can strengthen relationships and improve collaboration and overall team performance.

5.3. Classification of confidence-building exercises

Of the ways of defining these activities, we mention:

- Communication exercises (developed extensively in Chapter 6): These involve interactions that promote active listening, clear understanding of messages, and effective expression of ideas. Participants will be encouraged to communicate freely and share ideas, thoughts, and concerns without fear of judgment or excessive criticism (Miller, 2015). They can include role-playing, open-ended discussions, or activities where members must work together to solve problems.

- Challenging experiences: These involve outdoor or indoor activities such as rope adventures, orienteering, physical challenges, or other team tasks that require collaboration and mutual trust.
- Creative activities (developed extensively in Chapter 8): By working together on a creative project, such as painting, sculpting, or building an object, team members can develop trust through collaboration and individual contributions.
- Constructive feedback and evaluation (developed extensively in Chapter 9): Taking the time to give and receive feedback is essential to building trust. This should be done in a positive and constructive way, encouraging personal and collective development.
- Problem-solving activities (developed extensively in Chapter 8): These involve presenting teams with challenges or difficult scenarios that require collaboration and finding solutions together.
- Physical confidence exercises: Activities such as games where one team member relies on others to push their physical limits can build confidence and enhance team spirit.
- Emotional connection-building activities: These can include exercises to share personal experiences, emotion-based teambuilding activities, or other activities that help team members connect on a deeper level.
- Leadership skills development sessions (developed extensively in Chapter 8): Encouraging each member to take responsibility and develop their leadership skills can help build trust in the team.

It is important that these activities are tailored to suit the specific needs, dynamics, and goals of the team (Bloom et al., 2003; Siemens, 2010). It is also crucial that all activities are conducted in a positive and respectful manner to create a safe environment for all participants (Lacerenza et al., 2018).

Bee & Bee (1998) consider cultivating the opportunity to give and receive constructive feedback essential to developing trust among team members in teambuilding activities.

5.4. Examples of trust games

Activity 1: Trust in the line

Rules of conduct: A start and finish line are drawn. At the start signal, the first person from each team sits on the ground, parallel to the starting line, lying on their back with their hands out to the sides. The second person jumps over the first and sits next to them in the same position so that their toes touch. The game continues until the entire team crosses the finish line.

Poses of this application can be seen in Figure 5.1.

Figure 5.1. Trust in the line.

Activity 2: Forward the person

Context: This game involves building mutual trust and supportive relationships between team members. The game involves moving the participants on their arms. The game can be played outdoors and indoors.

Rules of conduct: Participants sit in a supine position with hands extended upward, supporting the volunteer's body on their palms, and passing it to a finish line located behind the furthest team member. After the first member has passed the body of the volunteer forward, they rise and move to a new catch and pass position at the head of the formation, in the direction of passing the volunteer. The other members will do the same in order after passing the body of the volunteer. The exercise is even more effective the more members it includes.

Poses of this application can be seen in Figure 5.2.

Figure 5.2. Forward the person.

Variants: The movement of the volunteer is done by rolling the participants' bodies sideways on the ground, so that the volunteer's body moves towards the finish line.

Activity 3: The willow in the wind

Context: This is a classic exercise in teambuilding activities aimed at developing trust and collaboration in a team. This game involves building mutual trust and supportive relationships between team members. It is important that the safety and comfort of the participants are a priority in this game. It is essential that there is an atmosphere of mutual respect and trust between team members for this exercise to be beneficial and to help build relationships and trust within the team. Additionally, this game may require adaptations based on participants' needs and comfort, and the facilitator should closely monitor progress and provide support and guidance as needed.

Rules of conduct: Participants gather in a circle, and one person sits in the center of the circle. The person inside relaxes and lets herself fall back, her body stretched out, and the other team members catch her in their arms. Communication is the key to this exercise. The person being caught must be comfortable and confident that the other team members will support them safely. At the same time, the people holding it must be careful and offer their support depending on the comfort level of the participants; the exercise can be adapted to increase the degree of difficulty. This can mean lifting the person up and lowering them with control, adding the element of confidence and extra support.

Poses of this application can be seen in Figure 5.3.

Figure 5.3. The willow in the wind.

Variants: The game can be played outdoors and indoors. A variant of the game is for the volunteer to be blindfolded.

Activity 4. Falling into the void

Context: This is a basic exercise for building mutual trust within a team. Organizing in a responsible and safe way, communication and mutual respect are priorities during its implementation.

Rules of conduct: This exercise involves a person falling backwards, backwards, into the arms of colleagues standing in a row, who are positioned so that they can safely support the falling person.

Methodical guidelines: To organize this activity safely and efficiently, some important aspects will be considered:

- Facilitators will ensure that all participants are properly trained and clearly understand the procedure and safety of this exercise. There must be a level of trust and cooperation between all involved.
- Team members who will catch the falling person must be prepared and confident in their abilities. Facilitators will ensure that team members are prepared to properly grab the person and provide the necessary safety.
- It is recommended to choose a suitable surface for this exercise, which is soft and ensures that there are no dangerous objects around that could cause any danger in the event of an accidental fall.

- It is important to respect the comfort and limits of the participants. If someone does not feel comfortable doing this exercise, they should not be forced to participate. An environment in which each person can openly express their desires and limitations will be encouraged.

Poses of this application can be seen in Figure 5.4.

Figure 5.4. Falling into the void.

Activity 5: The circle of poppies

This is a game of confidence that also involves the animator's attention to avoid accidents. The game can be played outdoors and indoors.

Rules of conduct: The participants sit in a circle, facing inward, holding hands. By moving backwards, the circle is made as large as possible by stretching out the hands. Each participant is assigned a number (1 or 2), and at the animator's command, one of the numbers bends forward or backward. Possible commands are:

- 1 forward and 2 backward
- 1 backward and 2 forward
- 1 and 2 backward

During the application, each member of the team keeps their body stretched (rigid) and their feet in the same place and glued together.

Poses of this application can be seen in Figure 5.5.

Figure 5.5. The circle of poppies.

Activity 6: Treasure recovery

Context: The group is behind a line drawn on the ground. A volunteer will try to recover an object placed at about 2 m from the line on the ground, without touching the ground between the object and the line. As this cannot be done under normal conditions, the group will find solutions to support the volunteer through different methods.

Rules of conduct: The group will try to support the volunteer by counterbalancing their weight with the help of grips chained to the volunteer's arms, legs, or body. During the exercise, they will not have to touch the space between the object and the line, being metaphorically called "steep" or "watercourse."

Poses of this application can be seen in Figure 5.6.

Materials needed: Any lightweight object (glove, hat, scarf, cone, etc.).

Figure 5.6. Treasure recovery.

Activity 7. Stretch the string

Context: The participants are arranged in a circle, holding a circular string in their hands, depending on the dimensions of the circle. By extending the arms, perform a backward drop with the body rigid, without moving the feet from the ground.

Rules of conduct: Participants must cooperate so that the balance of the circle is maintained. When the members place their weight back, they bend their knees, getting as close to the floor as possible. The aim is to keep the circle in balance.

Materials needed: 8–10 m long rope or climbing rope.

Poses of this application can be seen in Figure 5.7.

Variants: Participants hold only one hand on the string, performing the same challenge.

Activity 8. Spiderweb

Context: Spiderweb is a teambuilding exercise that involves passing team members through a network of strings or ropes arranged to resemble a spider web. The purpose of this exercise is to develop trust, but at the same time, it also acts to encourage collaboration, communication, and strategy building as a team. The goal of the team is to successfully navigate through this "spiderweb," one through each eye of the web, without touching the strings and without breaking the "web."

Rules of organization and conduct: An open space can be used where strings or ropes are stretched at different heights and angles to create a structure like

Figure 5.7. Stretch the string.

a spider's web. This structure should allow enough space for participants to pass under or over the strings without touching them. Two trees about 3–4 m apart, or the side bars of a handball/soccer goal, can be successfully used.

The string fabric must describe as many holes as there are team members.

Methodical indications: The team must think of a strategy by which all members will have to escape to the other side of the spider's web so that each hole is used only once. The passage of the members will have to respect the rule of not touching the spider's web, and the game will sometimes require the passage of some teammates on the arms through the more difficult spaces to approach (smaller or higher, etc.). It is important that facilitators ensure a safe environment and monitor the activity to avoid injury and ensure a positive experience and valuable learning for all participants.

Poses of this application can be seen in Figure 5.8.

Materials needed: string and fixed pillars.

Activity 9: The pyramid

This game involves building a human pyramid, where team members work together to establish a stable and secure structure. It is essential to ensure a safe

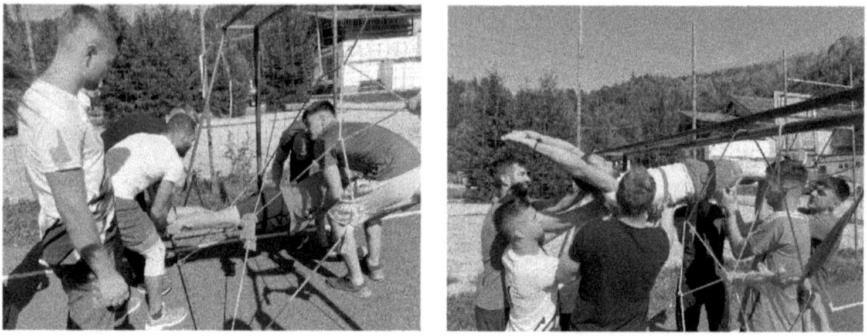

Figure 5.8. Spiderweb.

and positive experience for all participants and to highlight the importance of teamwork and mutual support in achieving common goals.

Rules of organization and conduct: The exercise requires clear instructions and competent design from the facilitators. They will divide the participants into balanced teams and ensure that each team has a leader or coordinator to guide them in setting up the pyramid.

Each team must discuss and plan how they will build the pyramid. This may involve choosing a base strategy, coordinating positions, and moves to form the upper levels of the pyramid. The team starts building the pyramid according to the agreed plan and strategy.

It is important to have clear communication and pay attention to safety while building the structure.

Methodical indications: While building the pyramid, there must be special attention to the safety of all participants. It is crucial that everyone feels comfortable and safe during the exercise.

Bibliography

Anderson, L. A., Midura, D. W., & Glover, R. D. (2019). *Team Building Through Physical Challenges*. Human Kinetics Publishers.

Avalos-Bevan, B., & Bascopé, M. (2017). Teacher Informal Collaboration for Professional Improvement: Beliefs, Contexts, and Experience. *Education Research International*.

Bee, R., & Bee, F. (1998). *Constructive Feedback*. CIPD Publishing.

Bloom, G., Stevens, D., & Wickwire, T. (2003). Expert Coaches' Perceptions of Team Building. *Journal of Applied Sport Psychology 15*(2), 129–43.

Burm, S., Boese, K., Faden, L., DeLuca, S., Huda, N., Hibbert, K., & Goldszmidt, M. (2019). Recognising the Importance of Informal Communication Events in Improving Collaborative Care. *BMJ Quality & Safety 28*(4), 289–95.

Depping, A. E., Mandryk, R. L., Johanson, C., Bowey, J. T., & Thomson, S. C. (2016, October). Trust Me: Social Games Are Better than Social Icebreakers at Building Trust. In Proceedings of the *2016 Annual Symposium on Computer-Human Interaction in Play* (pp. 116–29).

Dyer Jr, W. G., Dyer, J. H., & Dyer, W. G. (2013). *Team Building: Proven Strategies for Improving Team Performance*. John Wiley & Sons.

Engebø, A., Klakegg, O. J., Lohne, J., Bohne, R. A., Fyhn, H., & Lædre, O. (2022). High-Performance Building Projects: How to Build Trust in the Team. *Architectural Engineering and Design Management 18*(6), 774–90.

Everhart, R., Elliott, K., Pelco, L. E., Westin, D., Briones, R., & Peron, E. (2016). *Empathy Activators: Teaching Tools for Enhancing Empathy Development in Service-Learning Classes.*

Hakanen, M., Häkkinen, M., & Soudunsaari, A. (2015). Trust in Building High-Performing Teams: Conceptual Approach. *Electronic Journal of Business Ethics and Organization Studies 20*(2).

Lacerenza, C. N., Marlow, S. L., Tannenbaum, S. I., & Salas, E. (2018). Team Development Interventions: Evidence-based Approaches for Improving Teamwork. *American Psychologist 73*(4), 517.

Michalec, B., Schneider, J. M., & Mackenzie, M. (2021). Teaching Empathy in an Interprofessional Setting with a Focus on Decategorization: Introducing I-Team. *Journal of Interprofessional Education & Practice 22*, 100395.

Miller, B. C. (2015). *Quick Team-Building Activities for Busy Managers: 50 Exercises that Get Results in Just 15 Minutes*. HarperChristian + ORM.

Robbins, M. (2018). *Bring Your Whole Self to Work: How Vulnerability Unlocks Creativity, Connection, and Performance.* Hay House, Inc.

Siemens, L. (2010). The Potential of Grant Applications as Team Building Exercises: A Case Study. *Journal of Research Administration 41*(1), 75–91.

Tseng, H. W., & Yeh, H. T. (2013). Team Members' Perceptions of Online Teamwork Learning Experiences and Building Teamwork Trust: A Qualitative Study. *Computers & Education 63*, 1–9.

CHAPTER 6

Communication and Collaboration Activities

Daniel Roşu, Bogdan Cioabă, Diana Lefter, Lavinia Geambei, and Maria-Teodora Geambei

Summary: In this chapter, we propose to address the paradigms and communicational aspects within the teambuilding activities. We start from a theoretical foundation, from a linguistic perspective, of the three types of communication—verbal, non-verbal, and paraverbal—and we show that the communication process, through its tripolar structure: sender, message, receiver, involves not only coding, the transmitter's own activity, but also active listening, in the decoding process, which involves the receiver. Furthermore, we demonstrate the connections between the communication process and teambuilding activities, emphasizing that achieving effective communication is essential for team dynamics and cohesion. The activities presented in the second part have as their main component communication, which proves that the premise from which we started is confirmed.

Keywords: Communication, collaboration, active listening, team, cohesion

Teambuilding is a process that aims to increase cohesion between participants, get to know them better, create a common state of trust, increase motivation, and promote cooperation. Also, one of the main components of such an activity is communication *in presentia*, a deficient feature of the modern man surrounded by high technology.

Therefore, in this chapter, we will approach the concept of communication from a linguistic and communicational perspective, using the classic taxonomy: verbal communication, non-verbal communication, paraverbal communication (Benveniste, 1966, 1974; Sfez, 1993). In the first part of the text, we will make a brief presentation of the concept of communication, with the types stated above, insisting on the essential role of communication in an extra-linguistic activity, that of teambuilding.

In the second part of the text, we propose several types of teambuilding activities in which the communication element (in its various forms) is essential, thus demonstrating that the complex process of communication is an unavoidable component of teambuilding activities and that the three ways of communication are they are in a perfect symbiosis, contributing to the efficiency, and cohesion of the team. Communication, involving verbal–non-verbal complementarity, is essential in the business environment for creating and consolidating performance. Triadic process involving the pole of production, the pole of reception, and the message—transmitted through verbal and/or non-verbal channel—communication implies the existence or, in its absence, the construction of a communication code shared by both poles and of a common encyclopedic science. Building effective communication in the business environment is essential for achieving team cohesion, and teambuilding meetings can prove to be a conducive setting for finding ways to communicate effectively and building common knowledge of the world.

Usually, these activities are organized by the business environment and with a recreational purpose, but the real reason for these meetings is to increase work productivity and, implicitly, to increase the profit of companies and employees.

Teambuilding activities aim to create a culture of collaboration and mutual trust, so communication has a primary role. Incidentally, all three functions of communication established by Gamble & Gamble (1993) are considered in these activities, with emphasis on the second one, which aims *to develop consistent relationships with others*. Ion Ovidiu Pânişoara, in *Comunicarea eficientă* (Pânişoara, 2006, pp. 40–1), summarizes these functions, as they are described by the two researchers:

The first function refers to *understanding and knowledge*. Thus, communication supports both a better self-knowledge and the knowledge of others. Moreover, these two types of knowledge are interdependent: when we know others in the communication process, we simultaneously know our own being, we learn how others influence us and the extent to which we influence them, in turn. We can say that we look into the eyes of others as in a mirror; sometimes the mirror does not reflect as it should, it distorts, and yet we need it to know how we look.

A second function of communication aims at *developing consistent relationships with others*. It is not enough to develop our own selves in relation to others and to know them. We need communication, we need relationships through which we can share our reality with others, to build together the meanings of the reality that surrounds us. Through this, communication obviously also fulfils a function of socialization of the person.

The third function concerns the dimension of *influence and persuasion* of communication. Through communication, we can influence others to be part of our activity to achieve certain goals. This function develops the idea of collaboration and joint effort, perspectives that communication creates in human interaction.

That is why we believe that a short theoretical exposition regarding the concept of communication is necessary first.

6.1. Defining the concept of communication

Communication is a complex process, related to the specifics of the human being, a major social phenomenon, one of the most important forms of manifestation of the interactions between the organization and the environment, a means to establish and maintain various types of social relations, therefore it is "a process by which a transmitter transmits information to the receiver through a channel, with the aim of producing certain effects on the receiver" (coord. Drago & Boroli, 2004, p. 24).

Communication competence is a key competence that develops not only during schooling, but throughout life.

Being a process characterized by *plurality*, the act of communication involves *the addresser* (the person who produces signs, transmits information) and *the addressee* (the person who interprets the signs, receives information). The other constitutive elements of the act of communication are *the message* (the information transmitted), *the common code* (the communication system based on which the messages are built), *the channel* (the medium through which the information is transmitted), *the referent* (the theme of the message), *the context* (the circumstances of the communication).

Considering these factors of the act of communication, several *functions of communication (language)* have been established.

The famous linguist Roman Jakobson (1963) proposes a taxonomy of communication functions after focusing on one of the six factors of the act of communication:

- The expressive or emotional function, centered on the sender.
- The call or conative function, centered on the receiver.
- The poetic function, centered on the message.
- The metalinguistic function, centered on the code.

- The phatic function, centered on the channel.
- The referential function, centered on the referent.
- The cognitive or reflexive function, centered on the context.

We must mention that in the same act of communication, several functions of language can be manifested, but some are dominant in certain sequences.

Communication with words is *verbal communication*, based on natural languages. Depending on the type of transmission channel, verbal communication has two forms: *oral communication* and *written communication*. The communication tool is *the word*, a combination of a *signifier* (its form) and a *signified* (its meaning). Be it oral or written, *the message* is called an *utterance*, and *the code* used is the linguistic system produced by an *addresser* or *speaker* to an interlocutor or *addressee.*

In teambuilding activities, *oral communication* is predominant, sometimes it is exclusively used. Therefore, we will insist on it.

The features that define the specificity of oral communication are:

- Linguistic features (*verbal communication*).
- Non-linguistic features (*non-verbal communication*).
- Paralinguistic features (*paraverbal communication*).

Since the contemporary theories of communication are influenced by disciplines such as linguistics, pragmatics, psychology, sociology, anthropology, and philosophy, today they ensure an important place for non-verbal and paraverbal communication, understanding that, in fact, human communication is a complex process in which vocal-acoustic and visual elements are combined.

Therefore, communication is an essential aspect in building interpersonal relationships, and in the context of teambuilding, this is the major objective. When conducting training and teambuilding activities, effective communication is crucial to achieve set goals and create a culture of collaboration and mutual trust.

Starting from this premise, we will explore the importance of verbal, non-verbal, and paraverbal communication in the teambuilding process and their impact on the results obtained, also proposing examples of activities that contribute to the creation of a solid team.

6.2. Verbal communication in teambuilding

Verbal communication represents the transmission of information with the help of words, the linguistic features standing out at the phonetic, morphological, syntactic, and lexical levels. In the context of teambuilding, verbal communication can be achieved through speeches, questions, games, feedback, and other forms of word-based interaction. There are some key aspects of verbal communication to consider in teambuilding activities:

***Clarity and consistency of messages*:** For the communication process to be effective, the messages transmitted must be clear, concise, and easily understood by all participants. Using plain language and avoiding technical or ambiguous jargon are important aspects of ensuring effective verbal communication.

***Active listening*:** Listening carefully and responding appropriately to the messages of other team members are essential aspects of verbal communication in teambuilding. Active listening demonstrates respect and interest in the perspective of others, helping to build trust and improve team relationships.

In teambuilding activities, both forms of oral communication can be used: *dialogue*, *monologue*, but it is important to use them as efficiently as possible.

In the paperwork "Comunicare ficţională şi nonficţională" (Artagea & Tanef, 2005, p. 42), the rules of an effective dialogue are established:

- We take over the role of addresser when the pre-speaker has finished his intervention.
- We take over the role of addresser when we know that there is no one else before us who wants to intervene.
- In the case of a dialogue between people we do not know, we assume the role of addresser, asking for permission to participate in the discussion.
- The intervention of an addresser must not be long.
- The message must be appropriate to the context of the dialogue and to the purpose of the addresser's intervention.

And to support an effective monologue, it is necessary to follow a few rules:

- Before the monologue, we clearly establish the ideas we intend to promote (it is recommended that there are no more than three).

- We select the arguments suitable for each idea.
- We order the arguments according to their importance, thinking about the weight we can give them depending on the time available.
- We fit into the allotted time.

6.3. Non-verbal communication in teambuilding

Non-verbal communication, also called *body language* or *analogical communication*, refers to the transmission of information through facial expressions, gestures, head position, visual contact, and other non-verbal signals. "Non-verbal communication involves the sum of stimuli (except for verbal ones) present in the context of a communication situation, generated by the individual and containing a potential message" (Chiru, 2003, p. 32). Furthermore, "All forms of non-verbal communication messages have their own temporalities, beginnings, and endings, startings and stoppings, zeros and ones, befores and afters, faster and slower, and so forth. Verbal messages, too, have major temporal features. We could not possibly communicate without human temporality" (Littlejohn & Foss, Eds., 2009, p. 97).

The knowledge and appropriate use of non-verbal communication elements are assets that develop self-confidence and the power of persuasion and generate positive relationships, empathy, leading to the success of a process.

Starting from the idea that non-verbal language and verbal language operate together, supporting each other in the process of oral communication, the authors of the paperwork *Comunicarea nonverbală: gesturile şi postura* (Chelcea et al., 2005, pp. 32–3) stated the axioms of non-verbal communication in close correlation with the axioms of verbal communication established by the representatives of the Palo Alto School.

These are:

- Non-verbal communication is phylogenetically and ontogenetically primordial.
- In direct interpersonal communication, it is not possible not to communicate non-verbally.
- Non-verbal communication represents an element in the human communication system and should not be analyzed independently of verbal communication.

- Non-verbal communication is multi-channel and is carried out through a system of signs and signals (discrete and analogue), codes and channels, and its global analysis is necessary.
- In non-verbal communication, the meaning of multi-channel transmitted signs must be contextualized and established in terms of probabilities.

Therefore, although it can often be underestimated, non-verbal communication plays a significant role in interpersonal relationships, and through teambuilding activities, participants can become aware of the importance and meaning of non-verbal signs, understanding that they have a strong emotional impact.

Relevant aspects of non-verbal communication include facial expressions and body language as well as eye contact and gestures.

6.3.1. Facial expressions and body language

Facial expressions and posture can convey emotions and attitudes that can influence team interactions.

All these non-verbal elements (mimicry, smile, laughter, look, body position) are very important. For example, posture is a way of relating, offering a lot of information related to the desire for communication, attitudes, emotions, education, affectivity, social hierarchy, etc.

We will further present four types of main postures that the authors of the paperwork *Comunicare ficțională și nonficțională* (Artagea & Tanef, 2005, p. 26) establish, to which partial postures are added.

The four main types of postures are:

- Of submission
- Of dominance
- Of rejection
- Of sharing

These main postures are composed of a series of *partial postures*, which strengthen or destructure the overall impression.

- *The approach or reception posture* is the typical body expression of two people meeting. Each one walks towards the other, with the torso

slightly inclined, the neck slightly stretched, the hand extended to the other, open as a sign of sharing.
- *The rejection or avoidance posture* is that of the individual who defends themselves (the specific position of the boxer who wants to avoid blows, of the fencer, etc.): with the torso bent to the back, with the hands raised in defense.

Posture highlights a certain attitude (Artagea & Tanef, 2005, p. 26). Thus:

- *The posture in contraction* signifies a submissive, shy, introverted attitude: head between the shoulders, slightly inclined, shoulders slumped, torso bent, elbows next to the body, feet together. The peri space is reduced.
- *The posture in extension* signifies a domineering attitude: chin and head raised, broad shoulders, open arms, feet apart, palms to the ground, impression of over-dimensioning.
- *The approach posture* demonstrates a participatory attitude: head forward, slightly elongated neck, bust bent outward, the posture proves interest in the interlocutor, the desire to communicate.
- *The rejection posture* proves an attitude of refusal: head turned, arms in the barrier, bust in profile, oblique gaze.

Any change in global posture is meaningful and allows the interlocutor's attitude to be quickly decoded.

Therefore, an open body position or a sincere smile can indicate trust and comfort, facilitating collaboration and building team relationships.

6.3.2. Eye contact and gestures

Looking means meeting and starting communication with the other. It can facilitate communication or block it in ambiguous situations. The look is loaded with meanings and has an extremely important role in strengthening interpersonal relationships. Like many of the non-verbal elements, the look is also culturally connoted. Thus, in European culture, when we communicate with the other, when we speak to him or when we listen to him, we maintain eye contact with him.

Analyzing the gaze, Dale C. Leathers establishes several functions of the ways of looking (Leathers, 1997, cited in Artagea & Tanef, 2005, p. 23):

- The function of attention, the interlocutors pay attention to each other or unilaterally.
- The regulatory function, which marks the beginning and end of communication.
- The power function, through which positive or negative emotions are manifested.

The function of forming the impression, which communicates the way in which the individual wants to be seen, is perceived.

- The persuasive function of increasing credibility by maintaining visual contact.

Therefore, maintaining appropriate eye contact and using gestures appropriately can reinforce verbal messages and express attention and involvement with others. Body movements or facial expressions have a primary role in elaborating the message. To strengthen this idea, in the paperwork *Comunicare ficțională și nonficțională* (Artagea & Tanef, 2005, p. 25), Bernard Rimé is mentioned, a researcher at the Catholic University of Louvain-la-Neuve, Belgium, who insists on the obvious relationship between the movements of the body and the cognitive aspect of language. The results of his experiments show the fact that man thinks better when moving than in a state of immobility. The richer and more nuanced their vocabulary, the more gestures they make when they speak or think intensely. Through teambuilding activities, participants learn to correctly decode their gestures and those of others, in order to transmit and receive the message correctly.

Direct eye contact and friendly gestures help to increase interpersonal bonds and develop trust within the team.

6.4. Paraverbal communication in teambuilding

Paraverbal communication refers to the way words are spoken, including tone of voice, rate of speech, volume, voice inflections (whispering, shrill, grunting, hissing), pauses, articulation of sounds, and other characteristics that can influence the understanding and impact of messages transmitted.

In the context of teambuilding, paraverbal communication has a significant influence on the atmosphere and group dynamics.

When the paraverbal elements appear intentionally, they have the role of highlighting different states of mind or drawing the interlocutor's attention to the essential aspects in the act of communication, or showing the sender's intention to establish effective communication with the other.

Here are some key elements of paraverbal communication:

- Voice tone and intonation: How the tone of voice is used can indicate emotions, moods, and different levels of confidence. A warm and empathetic tone can enhance the emotional connection between team members and encourage openness and effective communication.
- Pace and volume of speech: An appropriate pace and controlled volume of the voice can ensure clear communication and facilitate the understanding of the messages conveyed. Speaking too fast or too slowly, and the volume too low or too high, can affect the communication process and cause confusion.

Therefore, verbal, non-verbal, and paraverbal communication are interdependent and essential elements in the teambuilding process. Effective communication within the team facilitates, the creation of a harmonious working environment, improves interpersonal relationships, and contributes to the achievement of set goals. In this regard, it is important to pay attention to all aspects of communication, such as the clarity of verbal messages, the appropriate expression of emotions through non-verbal communication, and the correct use of paraverbal communication features.

6.5. Types of communication and collaboration activities in teambuilding

As shown by De Janasz et al. (2002), in teambuilding activities, teams can improve their communication and various internal processes, make better decisions, increase their creativity and morale to better respond to the competition. In addition, Labelle shows that the process of strengthening a team means gathering its members around a common goal, in a climate that favors communication, dynamism, and the pleasure of working (Labelle,

2001). It is known that similarities between people facilitate the creation of connections, and communication requires minimal effort (Rogers & Bhowmik, 1970).

The communication and collaboration activities have a recommended duration of about 60–90 min; they are designed to encourage team members to work together, improve their listening skills, understand others' needs and perspectives, and solve problems effectively. Among the types of communication and collaboration activities in teambuilding, we can mention:

- Active listening exercises: These involve activities where team members must listen carefully to the information provided and demonstrate correct understanding of it. Word games, information transfer exercises, or other similar activities can be used.
- Role-play and scenario simulations: These activities involve putting team members in fictional or real situations where they must interact and collaborate to solve a problem or achieve a specific goal.
- Team games and competitive activities (also presented in Chapter 10): These are games and exercises where team members must work together to achieve a common goal. This is where physical challenge games, strategy games, and the like come in.
- Trust-building exercises (also presented in Chapter 5): These activities involve situations in which team members must prove to each other that they can count on each other. These exercises can be physical in nature or based on tasks that require mutual trust.
- Strategic thinking exercises (also presented in Chapter 8): These are activities that emphasize the development of planning and strategy skills. Team members must collaborate to find creative and effective solutions to specific challenges.
- Brainstorming and problem-solving sessions (also presented in Chapter 8): These activities encourage team members to generate ideas, analyze options, and make collective decisions.
- Organizational culture-building activities: These can include sessions on sharing organizational values and goals, as well as exercises that promote group cohesion and identity.
- Simulations of work projects or activities: Team members can be involved in fictitious projects or exercises that reflect specific work

activities to improve collaboration and communication skills in a relevant context.

These activities are essential to develop an effective team based on trust, open communication, and effective collaboration. They should be selected based on the specific needs and goals of the respective team.

6.6. Examples of communication and collaboration activities

Activity 1. The telephone game or The broken telephone game

Context: This exercise involves relaying a piece of information or a phrase through a sequence of participants and highlights the importance of listening carefully and communicating clearly in a team. This exercise highlights how information can be distorted or misinterpreted as it is passed from one team member to another. It highlights the importance of active listening and clear communication to avoid misunderstandings within a team. It is an interactive and fun way to illustrate how important careful listening and accurate communication are in team collaboration.

Rules of conduct: Participants sit or stand next to each other in a row or circle. The organizer starts with a piece of information or a phrase and conveys it discreetly or whispering to the first participant in line. It is essential that the message is sent only once and not repeated. The first participant transmits the received information to the next in line, either by whispering in their ear or speaking in a low voice. This process continues throughout the chain of participants until the information reaches the last participant. The last participant speaks in public or writes down the message or phrase they heard. Finally, the initial information is compared with what reached the last participant.

Activity 2. Scenario game

Context: Organizers create a specific crisis or emergency scenario that requires resolution or decision-making within a limited time. This scenario can be related to the professional background of the participants, or it can be a fictitious scenario relevant to the field of activity.

Rules of conduct: Participants are assigned to different roles or teams that could exist in a similar real crisis or decision-making situation. These roles may include leaders, team members, subject matter specialists, communicators, customers, or other relevant roles. Participants are briefed on the crisis scenario and asked to interact, collaborate, and make decisions to solve the problem or manage the situation within a limited time. They must rely on available resources and communicate effectively to find solutions. Organizers or facilitators monitor the progress and interactions during the scenario. At the end, participants are brought together to discuss their experience, debate decisions made and highlight what worked well and what could be improved.

Activity 3: Minefield

Context: An area with free spaces is marked and objects (such as pieces of paper, circles drawn on the ground, or other small objects) representing "mines" are placed on the surface of the playing field. Participants are divided into teams of two, three or more depending on the size of the group and the requirements of the game.

Rules of conduct: The goal of the game is for team members to get through the "minefield" of objects without touching the "mines." Each "mine" is considered a danger zone, and if hit, the player must start over from the starting point. Depending on the version of the game, one team member is blindfolded, or the team must communicate verbally to get safely through the minefield. If the blindfold option is used, the blind partner must be guided through the minefield only with the help of his partner's voice cues. The sighted must give clear, precise, and concise directions on how to navigate their partner without hitting the "mines." At the same time, the navigator must trust and carefully follow the instructions received. After the first pair has crossed the minefield or reached a predetermined objective, the roles can be reversed so that each team member can navigate the minefield or provide directions.

Materials needed: Tracing elements, blindfolds and about 50 small objects.

Activity 4: The flying stick

Context: The "Flying Stick" activity not only emphasizes collaboration and communication, but also the creativity and adaptability of the team in finding an effective solution to keep the stick in the air.

Rules of conduct: Participants are divided into teams of several people, depending on the total number of participants. Each team sits in pairs, facing each other, with hands extended forward and index fingers extended. Between them the stick is placed on the fingers, which must either be maintained or transported to a distance set by the animator and placed on the ground. The basic rule is for participants to hold the stick only with their fingers under the stick and for all participants to always touch the stick. The team must work closely together, communicate, and coordinate movements to keep the stick in the air. Each team member could have a specific role or responsibility in carrying the baton. The team can experiment with different approaches and techniques to find the most effective method of making the stick hover in the air for as long as possible.

Materials needed: Similar long, thin, and light sticks, such as a wooden or plastic stick.

Activity 5: The caterpillar with eyes on the tail

Context: the game involves communication between a participant and the rest of the team forming a line, with the team having to follow a route. The goal of the game is for the team to find the most effective way to communicate.

Rules of conduct: The group is divided into two or more teams, each team chooses a leader who later leads the team along the route, being the only one not blindfolded. The participants must permanently maintain contact with the person in front (by touching the shoulders of the person in front). The team members must be guided only by the movements of the one in front, based on the commands transmitted verbally or non-verbally by the one behind. The route can be drawn with various objects or obstacles such as tables, chairs, sticks, etc.

An example of this application can be seen in Figure 6.1.

Materials needed: Blindfolds, small objects and improvised obstacles that do not endanger the physical integrity of the participants.

Activity 6: Team skiing

Context: The team is arranged in column, seated in the stand, on two devices that imitate a pair of skis. Each participant has both feet posted on "skis." The skis will also be handled by means of hangers at the level of the legs and with the help of strings at the level of the hands.

Rules of conduct: Depending on the length of the device, groups of 4–7 participants can be formed, who will have to, in tandem, move the

Figure 6.1. The caterpillar with eyes on the tail.

devices, imitating alternative walking on skis. The participants will have to simultaneously lift the same leg and make the same movement with the arms, so that they can advance on the "skis" covering a certain distance. Your team should ideally coordinate by executing the same movement simultaneously.

An example of this application can be seen in Figure 6.2.

Materials needed: The skis will be made from pieces of board with a thickness of about 2 cm and a length of about 3–4 m, on which are placed leg fastening systems in the form of bracelets and attached strings, about 50–80 cm long for working with arms.

Activity 7: The collective letter

Context: The group will have to use as a team a writing/painting/coloring object supported simultaneously by all participants through an ad hoc built device. Thus, each member has equal access to handling the object through an extension cord.

Figure 6.2. Team skiing.

Rules of conduct: The device will be made through a collective idea, any tool/variant for remote handling of the writing object being accepted.

The team will have to transcribe a word, make a drawing upon request, or color an image in the most attractive way possible, the competition aiming at the aesthetics of that work.

An example of this application can be seen in Figure 6.3.

Materials needed: One or more pens/felt-tip pens/markers, straight wooden or plastic sticks, rulers, scotch tape.

Activity 8: Build in the dark!

Context: The game optimizes verbal communication, imagination, and tactile sense by excluding the visual analyzer. On a square field with a side of about 4–5 m, the elements of 3–4 puzzles are randomly scattered, which assembled in a certain order constitute 3–4 similar shapes required by the game. The optimal strategy of each team is to find and use the right resources at hand before they are used by the other teams, which act simultaneously.

Figure 6.3. The collective letter.

Observance of the rule of action inside the field only with eyes closed on the basis of fair play is essential.

Rules of conduct: The game is ideally played in 3–4 teams of 5–7 members each. At any moment of the game, there is one player from each team on the field. One by one, one member enters the field with his eyes closed, trying to perform a single maneuver of coupling two pieces, under the verbal guidance of the rest of the team, after which he returns to one side of the field, preferably as far as possible, with his eyes closed. The next player who must enter the game makes a mental plan with his eyes open on the edge of the field, then closes his eyes and moves to the work started by his team, takes a necessary piece (scattered from the beginning of the game on the field), having the freedom to build further with a single mounting maneuver. This can be done based on their own memorization skills or with the help of the team, with whom they communicate verbally. The game continues until one of the teams completes the given shape.

An example of this application can be seen in Figure 6.4.

Materials needed: 3–4 identical puzzles with large pieces.

Figure 6.4. Build in the dark!

Activity 9. Session on sharing organizational values and objectives

Context: The team gathers to discuss and clarify organizational values and goals. Each member is encouraged to share what each value means to them and how they fit into it.

Rules of conduct: Participants are divided into small groups and asked to discuss and identify the most important values for the organization. These groups can brainstorm and develop short presentations about their most significant values.

Activity 10. The time machine

Context: "Time Machine" is a role-playing game in which participants have to use their imagination and communication skills to create a story full of action and adventure. The purpose of the game is to explore the theory that time travel can change the future and see how past actions can impact the present.

Rules of conduct: The team must imagine that they have found a time machine that will allow them to travel back in time and change events. Participants must create a story in which their past actions have an impact on the present. As time allocations, we recommend that the team have 5 min to prepare and 6 min to present the constructed story. Participants must work together to create a coherent and interesting story. During the third visit to the past, the team must change one thing that will bring the present back to normal.

Variants: Instead of traveling to the past, participants could travel to the future and explore how their actions in the present can impact the future.

Activity 11: The story

Context: "The story" is an activity that encourages collaboration and creativity among participants. Each participant will take turns saying a sentence to create a story with a beginning, middle, and end.

Rules of conduct: The participants will sit in a circle or in a line, and one of them will start the story with a sentence. Then the next participant will say a sentence that continues the story, and so it will continue in turn. The story must be coherent and make sense. There is no limit to the number of sentences each participant can say, but they must be consistent with the story.

Variants: Some additional restrictions or challenges can be introduced in the game to make it more interesting. For example, a time limit can be set for each sentence, or participants can be asked to include a specific word or theme in their sentence. Also, the activity can gain competitiveness, dividing the group into teams that will create their own story, which will be presented and appreciated successively.

Activity 12: Superheroes

Context: The present activity is an improvization game in which the members of a team have to present a skit illustrating a reversed day in the life of some superheroes, starting in the evening and ending in the morning of the same day. They must include three good things done by superheroes in the skit, which can include stopping a crime or catching a criminal, helping a disadvantaged person, and saving the city from an outside force. Participants are encouraged to do their performances in reverse and speak in reverse to make the performance more interesting.

Rules of conduct: Participants have to prepare a skit depicting a reversed day in the life of superheroes, starting in the evening and ending in the morning of the same day.

Variants: Change the order of the day's events, such as presenting a day that starts with its middle and ends with its beginning. Choose other good superhero activities like rescuing a stray animal, preventing a natural disaster, or helping someone find their way in life.

Activity 13: Story cards

Context: The story cards activity is a fun activity that engages the creativity and imagination of the participants in a group. Each player chooses a card with an adjective or noun written on it and uses the written word in a story. Then the next player chooses another tile and continues the story. The aim of the game is to create a coherent and interesting story while using the words on the chosen cards.

Rules of conduct: Participants will sit in a circle or line when the presentation is to be made on a stage. Word sheets (adjectives and nouns) will be prepared. The first participant will choose a card and use the word noted in a story. The next participant will continue the story using the word written on the card they chose. Each participant will try to present their improvization as quickly as possible, or they have a maximum of 1 min to continue the story. The aim of the game is to create a coherent and interesting story, using the words on the chosen cards.

Variants: The game can be adapted to the topic or theme of the session so that the words on the cards are related to the topic. Instead of words, cards can contain short phrases or questions, and players must continue the story by starting from those phrases or answering the questions.

Bibliography

Artagea, A. M. & Tanef, L. (2005). *Comunicare Ficțională* și *Nonficțională.* Gabriel.

Benveniste, E. (1966, 1974). *Problèmes de Linguistique Générale*. Gallimard.

Chelcea, S., Ivan, L. & Chelcea, A. (2005). *Comunicarea Nonverbală: Gesturile* și *Postura*. Comunicare.ro.

Chiru, I. (2003). *Comunicarea Interpersonală*. București. Tritonic.

De Janasz, S. C., Dowd, K. O. & Schneider, B. Z. (2002). *Interpersonal Skills in Organizations*. McGraw-Hill.

Drago, M. & Boroli A. (coord.) (2004). *Enciclopedia de Filosofie* şi *Ştiinţe Umane*. All.

Gamble, T. K. & Gamble, M. (1993). *Communication Works*. McGraw-Hill.

Jakobson, R. (1963). Essais de Linguistique Générale. *Les Éditions de Minuit.*

Labelle, G. (2001). *Une Équipe du Tonnerre: Découvrez le Processus de Consolidation D'équipes de Travail*. Editions Transcontinental inc. Fondation de 1 'Entrepreneurship.

Littlejohn, S. W. & Foss, K. A. (ed.) (2009). *Encyclopedia of Communication Theory*. SAGE Publications, Inc.

Pânişoară, I. O. (2006). *Comunicarea Eficientă*, ediţia a III-a. Polirom.

Rogers, E. M. & Bhowmik, D. K. (1970). Homophily-Heterophily: Relational Concepts for Communication Research. *The Public Opinion Quarterly 34*(4).

Sfez, L. (dir.) (1993). *Dictionnaire critique de la communication*. PUF.

Leadership and Decision-Making Activities

Daniel Roşu, Valentina Ştefănică, Sebastian Enache, and Florin Cojanu

Summary: This chapter refers to the effective combination of leadership and decision-making in teambuilding activities, which can essentially contribute to strengthening the team, improving communication, and promoting a healthy organizational culture.

Regarding leadership, the important elements refer to three instances: Directing—guiding the team towards achieving common objectives, encouraging collaboration; Inspiration—motivating team members, cultivating a positive and confident environment; Effective communication—clearly conveying directions and expectations, active listening, encouraging open dialogue.

Decision-making in teambuilding refers to the following three perspectives: Consultation—involving team members in the decision-making process to collect diverse perspectives; Objective analysis—evaluating available information and options in an equidistant and unbiased way; Taking responsibility—accepting the consequences of decisions and encouraging the involvement of team members in their implementation.

Keywords: Directing, inspiring, consulting, objective analysis, assuming responsibility, accepting the consequences of decisions

Leadership and decision-making activities in teambuilding are exercises and interactions planned to develop leadership and coordination skills and to improve team members' ability to make effective and informed decisions (Khan & Wajidi, 2019; Hedlund, 2017; Doyle, 2004). These activities encourage members to take responsibility, guide the team and make choices for the benefit of the group (Kuponiyi, 2008; Stoller, 2004; Pelican et al., 2021).

7.1. The importance of leadership and decision-making activities

Effective leadership in teambuilding activities is based on a combination of communication skills, listening, team involvement, and the ability to make wise and adaptable decisions, all of which are focused on achieving common team goals.

Effective leadership in teambuilding activities involves the ability to inspire, guide, and mobilize team members to achieve common goals. Decision making in this context requires a strategic and conscious approach to the needs and dynamics of the team. Among the recognized techniques that can effectively combine leadership and decision-making in teambuilding activities are:

- Clear communication of goals: An effective teambuilding leader clarifies and communicates the goals of the activity in a way that motivates team members to collaborate. These goals should be inspirational, measurable, and relevant to motivate team members.
- Trust and transparency: A good leader creates an environment where team members feel free to share ideas and contribute to the decision-making process. Transparency and trust in the approach to decisions help strengthen team relationships.
- Active listening: An effective teambuilding leader can listen and understand the different perspectives of team members, considering the diversity of ideas in the decision-making process. A leader should be a good communicator, listen and provide feedback, creating an environment where team members feel free to share ideas and collaborate.
- Involve the team in decision-making: Encouraging the team to participate in the decision-making process can help them feel valued and more committed to meeting common goals. An effective leader encourages collaboration and interaction among team members by stimulating the exchange of ideas and approaches.
- Adaptability and flexibility: An effective teambuilding leader is open to change and adapt to team dynamics and circumstances. Flexibility in approaching decisions can build trust among team members.
- Delegation of responsibilities: A wise leader knows how to delegate tasks and responsibilities according to the skills and expertise of each team member, which contributes to their involvement and commitment. Group members will be encouraged to assume roles and make decisions.
- Evaluation and continuous learning: A crucial aspect of effective leadership is the ability to evaluate results, learn from experiences, and adjust future strategies to improve decision-making and team performance.

Effective leadership contributes essentially to maintaining and promoting a healthy organizational culture (Bergman et al., 2012; Ejimabo, 2015). This requires constant efforts from management and the entire team. A strong culture benefits not only employees, but also the long-term performance and success of the organization.

Salas (2004) claims that in terms of leadership, the important elements refer to three postures:

- Directing—guiding the team towards achieving common goals, encouraging collaboration.
- Inspiring—motivating team members, cultivating a positive and confident environment.
- Effective communication—clear transmission of directions and expectations, active listening, encouraging open dialogue.

Directing and guiding the team towards common goals is a crucial part of the leadership role in a collaborative work environment such as teambuilding activities. These aspects are fundamental to ensuring that team members are aligned and motivated to work together for shared success.

Inspiring and motivating team members is essential to cultivating a positive and confident work environment. An effective leader can exercise his inspiring and motivating skills in various ways to increase the commitment and performance of team members. Among the strategies used by a leader for inspiration and motivation in a work environment can be mentioned:

- Communicating a vision and purpose: An inspirational leader shares a clear and compelling vision for the team, highlighting the purpose and importance of the shared mission. This vision motivates and guides the team towards common goals.
- Encouraging autonomy and creativity: Give team members the freedom and flexibility to express their creativity in solving problems and completing tasks. Opportunities to demonstrate their abilities can motivate them to realize their potential.
- Providing positive and constructive feedback: Recognizing good efforts and performance is essential for motivating team members. Positive and constructive feedback encourages team members to continue to strive and develop.
- Modeling positive behavior: An inspirational leader serves as an example through their behavior and how they handle difficult

situations. A positive attitude and a constructive approach to problems can positively influence the team.

- Encouraging collaboration and team spirit: Fostering an environment where team members support each other, collaborate, and share knowledge and skills can strengthen team cohesion and motivation.
- Setting and sharing goals and rewards: Clearly defining goals and the rewards associated with achieving them can motivate the team to focus their efforts on achieving them.
- Ensuring a positive work environment: Fostering a work environment where team members feel safe, valued, and respected can significantly improve team morale and motivation.

Senaratne & Samaraweera (2015) argue that decision-making in teambuilding refers to the following three perspectives:

- Consultation—involving team members in the decision-making process to collect diverse perspectives.
- Objective analysis—evaluation of available information and options in an equidistant and impartial way.
- Taking responsibility—accepting the consequences of decisions and encouraging the involvement of team members in their implementation.

If the aspects related to objective analysis and assumption of responsibilities about the role and functions of consultation, we can deepen some important ideas.

Consulting team members in the decision-making process is an important and beneficial practice in cultivating a healthy organizational culture and a more complete approach to the problems or decisions to be made. Involving team members in the decision-making process through consultation brings diverse perspectives and can improve the quality of decisions. Reasons why consultation is crucial include the following:

- Diverse Perspectives: Consulting team members bring in multiple perspectives, experiences, and different approaches to problems or situations. This can lead to a better informed and more comprehensive decision.

- Commitment and Trust: Involving team members in the decision-making process can strengthen their trust and commitment to the organization because they feel that their opinions and contributions are valued and considered.
- Diverse Knowledge and Expertise: Each team member brings a unique set of knowledge, skills, and experience. Consulting them can bring to the surface ideas or solutions that might not have been thought of otherwise.
- Innovative solutions: Consultation can lead to the generation of innovative and creative solutions. By bringing different perspectives together, the team can find unconventional approaches and ingenious solutions to problems or challenges encountered.
- Improving the decision-making process: Through consultation, the decision-making process becomes more transparent and inclusive. This can improve shared understanding of the issues and decisions to be made.
- Shared responsibility: When team members are involved in the decision-making process, a sense of shared responsibility for the final decision can be created. This can contribute to greater commitment to the implementation of the decision.

7.2. Types of leadership and decision-making identification activities

Among the typical activities of identifying leadership and making decisions, Hoyle (2006) mentions:

- Leadership exercises: These activities involve putting team members in leadership roles where they must take responsibility and provide direction to others. They may include crisis simulations or projects where a leader must coordinate the team to achieve a common goal.
- Leadership role plays: These activities involve games where team members must assume leadership roles and interact with others effectively. These can range from mock meetings and negotiations to team problem-solving.
- Leadership skills development sessions: These may include presentations, workshops, or interactive discussions on various aspects

of leadership such as communication, delegation, motivation, and conflict management.
- Simulations of complex projects or scenarios: Team members are put in situations where they must plan, organize, and lead complex projects or activities. These exercises require quick and efficient decision-making.
- Delegation exercises: These activities emphasize the ability of leaders to distribute tasks and responsibilities fairly and effectively within the team.
- Feedback and Self-Assessment Sessions for Leaders: These activities encourage leaders to receive feedback from teammates and self-assess to identify their strengths and areas for improvement.
- Crisis simulations: These activities put leaders in front of critical scenarios in which they must make quick and effective decisions to manage difficult or unforeseen situations.
- Strategic planning activities: Team members are involved in activities that require strategic planning, formulating goals, and identifying the resources needed to achieve those goals.

These activities are essential to develop leadership skills and promote a culture of informed and effective decision-making within the team (Ellis & Kell, 2014; Hamdani, 2018). They should be tailored to the specific needs of the team and provide opportunities for practice and continuous development (Aga et al., 2016).

7.3. Examples of leadership and decision-making activities

Activity 1. Leadership in crisis situations

Context: Simulating a crisis situation in teambuilding activities can be a useful way to test a team's problem-solving, communication, and collaboration skills in a controlled environment. This can help strengthen the team's cohesion and ability to deal with difficult situations.

Scenario: A fictional team of explorers is on a trip to a remote mountain. During an unexpected storm, one of the team members is injured and cannot continue moving. The team must act quickly and efficiently to deal with the emergency and save their colleague.

Deployment of the simulation: Before the simulation, the participants are informed about the crisis scenario and the roles they will play within it. Each team member is given a specific role and information about the skills and resources they possess within the scenario.

The scenario begins with a presentation of the crisis, such as the storm, the team member's injury, and the difficult weather conditions. Participants are actively involved in solving the situation. The team must collaborate to make quick and effective decisions. These decisions may include establishing a plan of action, providing first aid to the injured, finding shelter or an escape route, and communicating with rescue teams or authorities.

Although effective communication and cooperation are essential during the simulation, the game is especially aimed at highlighting individuals (leaders) who can envision the most viable solutions and who assume coordination of activities and responsibilities. Against this background, participants must work together, share information, identify solutions, and act as a united team to overcome obstacles.

Activity 2. Role-playing game "In Search of the Leader"

Context: Conducting a leadership role play in teambuilding activities can be an interactive and engaging way to explore and develop the leadership skills of team members. This role play allows participants to experience different leadership roles and develop their skills in a safe and controlled environment.

The purpose of the game will be to highlight and develop the leadership skills of team members, as well as test decision-making, effective communication, and problem-solving skills in a simulated environment.

Rules of conduct: The participants are divided into equal groups, each group representing a team of explorers who must reach a safe place in a remote region. Each group has a designated leader.

Each group is given a set of challenges or tasks that simulate the obstacles or challenges they might encounter during their journey. These may include physical obstacles, communication problems, difficult decisions, or complex tasks to solve.

At each challenge or stage of the game, the leader of each group is changed. Each participant has a chance to be the leader for a certain period.

Importance of this game: The game puts pressure on leaders to make quick and effective decisions in varied and rapidly changing situations. Clear and concise communication is required between leaders and team members while solving problems or completing tasks.

Leaders must be able to involve their team members in the decision-making process and distribute tasks appropriately to achieve goals. The game emphasizes the ability to adapt to new and unexpected situations and changes that occur within simulated challenges.

Activity 3. Leadership Skills Development Session

Context: A leadership skills development session in teambuilding activities can be designed to provide participants with hands-on and interactive opportunities to improve their leadership skills in an interactive and safe environment.

Purpose of the session: To develop and strengthen the leadership skills of the participants in an interactive and collaborative environment, as well as a practical understanding of the key components of an effective leader and their application in team activities.

Rules of conduct: A leadership trainer/expert introduces the key concepts of effective leadership: communication, decision-making, delegation, motivation, problem-solving, and adaptability. Participants are encouraged to reflect on their own experiences, values, and traits that define a leader for themselves. The trainer/expert also presents case studies that present real or simulated leadership situations and discusses, analyzes, and identifies strategies and solutions to address them.

Importance of this activity: The session focuses on hands-on experiences that allow participants to practice their leadership skills in varied and real-life situations. Giving and receiving feedback is essential to identify strengths and areas for improvement in each participant's leadership skills.

Activities are designed to promote teamwork and collaboration, emphasizing the importance of leadership that encourages and supports the team. The session encourages continuous learning where participants continue to develop their leadership skills and apply the knowledge gained in everyday activities.

Activity 4. Simulation of complex projects or scenarios: "Saving Planet X"

Context: In a project or complex scenario simulation, the development of quick decision-making, problem-solving, and resource management skills in a pressing situation will be pursued.

Rules of conduct: Participants are informed that a "planetary emergency" requires the intervention of a team of specialists to save Planet X from an imminent disaster (e.g., a natural or technological threat, an ecological crisis, etc.).

Participants are divided into teams, each team representing a group of specialists with different skills (e.g., researchers, engineers, doctors, scientists, etc.). Each team is given a set of specific objectives or tasks related to the crisis of Planet X, such as identifying the source of the disaster, developing a rescue plan, collecting resources, etc.

Teams are subject to resource restrictions (time, money, materials, etc.) and are forced to collaborate and manage these limited resources to achieve their goals. Teams engage in complex activities that may include puzzle solving, brainstorming, model building, planning, and quick decision making to manage the crisis.

Facilitators monitor each team's progress and provide feedback during the activity.

An example of this application can be seen in Figure 7.1.

Figure 7.1. Saving planet X.

Importance of this activity: Simulating complex projects or scenarios in teambuilding activities can be an engaging and interactive way to develop teamwork, decision-making, and problem-solving skills in a simulated environment, giving participants hands-on experience and valuable.

Participants are put in situations that require quick and efficient decision-making with limited resources. Simulation provides opportunities for complex problem-solving and creative thinking to tackle difficult situations.

Activity 5: "Task Puzzle Relay" delegation exercise

Context: An effective delegation exercise in teambuilding activities can help participants understand the importance of delegating tasks, practice communication skills, and improve team relations.

Purpose of the activity: Developing delegation and task management skills, along with improving communication and collaboration within the team.

Rules of conduct: The participants are divided into equal teams, each team consisting of 4–6 members. A relatively simple puzzle is prepared, but it requires the collaborative effort of the entire team to be solved. This can be a physical puzzle or a digital one. Each team receives an identical set of puzzle pieces.

In each team, one member is designated as the "manager" or "leader." The manager/leader is given the task of assembling the puzzle while the other team members must assist them. The manager cannot touch the puzzle pieces. They can only communicate verbally with other team members. The other people on the team can manipulate the puzzle pieces, but they cannot see the final picture of the puzzle. The manager/leader must coordinate their team, assign specific tasks to team members, and provide clear instructions for assembling the puzzle without touching the pieces or seeing the final image.

Activity variants: It can be chosen to be a competition between teams to see who solves the puzzle the fastest, or it can be promoted to encourage collaboration, with the ultimate goal of the complete and correct assembly of the puzzle by all teams.

Methodical guidelines: The manager must provide clear and concise instructions to guide the team in solving the task, while the team must collaborate and coordinate to solve the task, despite the limitations imposed by the rules of the exercise.

An example of this application can be seen in Figure 7.2.

Figure 7.2. Task puzzle relay.

Importance of this activity: This hands-on delegation exercise allows participants to experience first-hand the importance of delegation, communication, and collaboration within a team, providing opportunities for learning, developing, and improving teamwork skills.

Activity 6. Feedback and self-assessment session for leaders called: "Reflection and Development in Leadership"

Context: A feedback and self-assessment session for leaders in teambuilding activities can be an effective way to encourage personal and professional development of leaders and improve their leadership skills.

Purpose of session: Provide feedback and self-assess leadership skills to identify strengths and areas for improvement. The session may also aim to develop individual action plans to increase performance and leadership skills.

Rules of conduct: Each leader completes a questionnaire or set of questions about their leadership skills, approaches, strengths, and areas they want to develop. Leaders receive "360-degree feedback" from teammates, co-workers, and superiors, in an anonymous or confidential manner, on how they are perceived in terms of their leadership skills and interactions with the team.

An interactive session is organized where the leaders discuss and analyze the results of the self-assessment and the feedback received. Emphasis is placed on identifying the commonalities and differences between one's own perception and the perception of others. Participants are encouraged to identify and note their strengths and areas where they wish to develop in terms of their leadership skills. Timelines and ways of tracking the progress of individual action plans are established. Support and resources are also provided to help leaders achieve their goals.

Importance of this activity: Following such a session, leaders are encouraged to be open in evaluating their own performance and to receive feedback from others without judgment or defensiveness. Creating a specific and detailed action plan that includes measurable goals and concrete steps to achieve those goals is a significant help to leaders. In the same context, leaders are responsible for implementing their action plans and for tracking progress towards improving leadership skills.

Methodical guidelines: The questionnaire or set of questions must be prepared by facilitators with skills in psychological sciences.

Activity 7: "How tall is Alfred?" Game

Context: Game "How tall is Alfred?" It is a leadership discovery game, but it can also be considered a strategy game or group fun. In the game, participants have to estimate the height of a fictional character named Alfred. The leader stands out in the team by his ability to organize and select information in a logical and precise way.

Rules of conduct: The participants are divided into 6 or 12 teams, with a variable number of people, who will be stationed around a workspace. Each team will receive two official tickets if the game is played in 6 teams or one official ticket if the game is played in 12 teams. In these notes, there will be useful information that can lead to finding out Alfred's height. The tickets will be well shuffled so that one team does not benefit from successive information.

Each team will designate at least 1 postman, that is, a person who has to hand over and collect valuable information tickets from another team. The goal of each team is to change as many official tickets as possible with the predetermined information and correctly calculate the impact of this information on the main question, "How tall is Alfred?"

During each trip made by the postman, only one ticket will be exchanged with the team he travels to.

Verbal communication will be kept to a minimum during the game.

The contents of the official tickets are as follows:

Ticket 1: Alina is 156 cm tall.
Ticket 2: George is 4 cm taller than Alina.
Ticket 3: Cristian is 5 cm shorter than George.
Ticket 4: Marian is the same height as Cristian.
Ticket 5: Alexandra is 7 cm shorter than Marian.
Ticket 6: Horea is 8 cm taller than Alexandra.
Ticket 7: Roxana is the same height as Horea.
Ticket 8: Ionuţ is 3 cm taller than Roxana.
Ticket 9: Ciprian is 6 cm shorter than Ionuţ.
Ticket 10: Florina is the same height as Ciprian.
Ticket 11: Andrei is 17 cm taller than Florina.
Ticket 12: Alfred is the same height as Andrei.

The correct answer is: Alfred's height is 170 cm.

The importance of this game: The game can be played for fun or as a competition, recording the time required to find out the truth by each team separately, with consequences in the evaluation of leadership.

Activity 8. "The Traffic Jam" Game

Context: The "Traffic Jam" game is a teambuilding activity that simulates a congested traffic situation, emphasizing leadership, communication, decision making, and team collaboration to manage difficult situations.

Rules of conduct: Participants are divided into teams (for example, teams of 5–10 people each). Each team is given a "road" space with colored strips marked to simulate roads and intersections.

Participants are instructed to simulate a busy city, and each team represents the traffic drivers. They have to direct the traffic (team participants) to avoid "traffic jams" and collisions.

Each team member has a specific role (traffic controller, spotter, intersection coordinator, etc.). Participants must actively communicate with each other, collaborate to find the best solutions, and avoid traffic "accidents."

Traffic is initiated (participants move on the marked colored lanes) and various traffic situations are simulated: traffic jams, road works, sudden changes of direction, etc.

An example of this application can be seen in Figure 7.3.

Figure 7.3. The traffic jam.

Materials needed: Open space or a room large enough to allow movement of participants, colored tapes (colored paper, masking tape, tapes stuck to the ground, etc.) to mark the "roads" or "traffic lanes."

Importance of this game: The team must communicate quickly and clearly to avoid collisions and traffic jams in simulated traffic by achieving effective communication. Participants must make quick decisions and find solutions to handle unexpected traffic situations by improving decision-making. The team must collaborate and coordinate actions to keep traffic flowing and avoid deadlock situations by improving collaboration and coordination.

Bibliography

Aga, D. A., Noorderhaven, N., & Vallejo, B. (2016). Transformational Leadership and Project Success: The Mediating Role of Team-Building. *International Journal of Project Management 34*(5), 806–18.

Bergman, J. Z., Rentsch, J. R., Small, E. E., Davenport, S. W., & Bergman, S. M. (2012). The Shared Leadership Process in Decision-Making Teams. *The Journal of Social Psychology 152*(1), 17–42.

Doyle, L. H. (2004). Leadership for Community Building: Changing How We Think and Act. *The Clearing House: A Journal of Educational Strategies, Issues and Ideas* 77(5), 196–201.

Ejimabo, N. O. (2015). An Approach to Understanding Leadership Decision Making in Organization. *European Scientific Journal 11*(11).

Ellis, M., & Kell, B. (2014). Development, Delivery and Evaluation of a Team Building Project. *Leadership in Health Services 27*(1), 51–66.

Hamdani, M. R. (2018). Learning How to be a Transformational Leader Through a Skill-Building, Role-Play Exercise. *The International Journal of Management Education 16*(1), 26–36.

Hedlund, E. (2017). Team Learning and Leadership in Multinational Military Staff Exercises. *Armed Forces & Society 43*(3), 459–77.

Hoyle, J. R. (2006). *Leadership and Futuring: Making Visions Happen*. Thousand Oaks: Corwin Press.

Khan, M. R., & Wajidi, A. (2019). Role of Leadership and Team Building in Employee Motivation at Workplace. *GMJACS* 9(1), 11.

Kuponiyi, F. A. (2008). Community Power Structure: The Role of Local Leaders in Community Development Decision Making in Ajaawa, Oyo State, Nigeria. *The Anthropologist 10*(4), 239–43.

Pelican, K., Blair, B., Adisasmito, W., Allen, I., Amir, V., Bazeyo, W., & Bender, J. (2021). One Health Leadership and Team Building Training. In One Health: *The Theory and Practice of Integrated Health Approaches* (pp. 184–96). Wallingford, UK: CABI.

Salas, E., Burke, C. S., & Stagl, K. C. (2004). Developing Teams and Team Leaders: Strategies and Principles. *Leader Development for Transforming Organizations: Growing Leaders for Tomorrow*, 325–55.

Senaratne, S., & Samaraweera, A. (2015). Construction Project Leadership Across the Team Development Process. *Built Environment Project and Asset Management* 5(1), 69–88.

Stoller, J. K., Rose, M., Lee, R., Dolgan, C., & Hoogwerf, B. J. (2004). Teambuilding and Leadership Training in an Internal Medicine Residency Training Program: Experience with a One-Day Retreat. *Journal of General Internal Medicine* 19(6), 692–7.

CHAPTER 8

Problem-Solving Activities

Bogdan Cioabă, Diana Lefter, Lavinia Geambei, and Maria-Teodora Geambei

Summary: In this chapter, we propose to address the topic of problem solving, a crucial element of a teambuilding program. We start from a theoretical foundation that shows that problem-solving activities are meant to provide team members with the opportunity to work together in a structured and collaborative way to identify and solve various challenges or obstacles, which can lead to significant improvements in team performance. Further, we show what the results and benefits of these activities are: developing teamwork skills, cultivating team spirit, developing decision-making skills, increasing mutual trust, resolving conflicts, and encouraging creativity and innovation. The activities presented in the second part have as their main component communication to solve problems, being structured according to the model: team size, duration, rules of conduct, and advantages.

Keywords: Problem-solving, team spirit, relational dynamics, creativity, innovation

Schein (Schein, 1969, 1999), one of the first authors to theorize and define the concept of teambuilding, believes that problem-solving activities are a category of formal or informal interventions that emphasize improving interpersonal relationships and clarifying the roles of members in the team. In this sense, teambuilding produces results, as it helps everyone to analyze, diagnose, and act on their own behavior, which will have beneficial effects on the group. Moreover, "Le teambuilding can also facilitate the resolution of conflicts within the company, increasing the motivation of collaborators while reducing employee turnover rates." Gotham City Gazette (12 Oct. 2023).

8.1. The importance of problem-solving activities

In addition, studies in the field have shown that problem-solving is more effective when done in groups. Thus, if teams are effectively supported, there is a tendency to improve the quality of work and creativity in finding solutions at the group level (Baldwin et al., 2008); (Sweeney & McFarlin, 2002). In this direction, Klein (Klein et al., 2009) cares about the effectiveness of teambuilding activities and solving group problems. It becomes obvious that "In a team in crisis, the members are no longer capable of managing the situation. Their reactions risk no longer being consistent as positions may diverge regarding the resolution paths to follow, and the usual benchmarks are lost, thus weakening the emotional balance of the team members." (Kauffman, 2015, p. 249).Extra-linguistic aspects such as emotional and spatiotemporal aspects are also very important in managing problem solving in a group: "The pursuit of a (crisis) project management approach and problem-solving techniques can be advantageously deployed, while considering aspects of the human dimension: emotional aspects, possible suffering, impacts on human relationships, etc. All these means must be long-term and internal and external, individual, and collective support means can be combined." (Kauffman, 2015, p. 257).

But, as the director of the Albus Conseil company, Charles-Henri Colonna shows (Colonna, 2017), the teambuilding activity should not be considered a credible alternative for solving problems, but rather a stage, maybe even a springboard, but not a remedy. In this sense, Moine (2002) considers reason to be paramount before emotionality and emphasizes the importance of interactive observation to understand the other, these being the prerequisites for progress in team cohesion.

8.2. Types of problem-solving activities

Teambuilding problem-solving activities are exercises and interactions designed to improve team members' analytical, strategic, and collaborative skills to effectively solve challenges and difficulties. The recommended duration of these activities is around 60–90 min. These activities encourage members to think creatively, identify innovative solutions, and work together to overcome obstacles. From the multitude of ways of problem-solving activities, we can mention:

Problem-solving scenarios: These activities involve presenting team members with complex scenarios or situations that require the identification and application of appropriate solutions. These can be real situations or simulations.

Puzzle games and riddles: These are activities that require logical and analytical thinking. Team members must work together to solve problems presented through puzzles or other similar challenges.

Complex project simulations: Team members are involved in activities that involve planning, organizing, and implementing a complex project. These exercises require identifying problems and finding appropriate solutions.

***Problem-solving role plays*:** These involve putting team members in specific roles within a simulation, where they must identify and solve problems in a given context.

***Prioritization and time management exercises*:** These activities encourage team members to assess and manage resources (such as time and priorities) to address issues effectively.

***Brainstorming and idea generation sessions*:** These activities encourage team members to come up with new and innovative ideas to address existing problems.

***Conflict simulation and resolution exercises*:** These activities focus on the team's ability to manage and resolve conflict in a constructive and effective manner.

***Cause and effect analysis activities*:** Team members are involved in activities that require identifying and understanding the underlying causes of a problem to develop effective solutions.

These activities are essential to develop problem-solving skills and foster a team spirit to successfully face challenges. They should be tailored to the specific needs of the team and provide opportunities for practice and continuous development.

8.3. Examples of problem-solving activities

Their goal is to help colleagues work better as a team, solve problems, achieve goals, and achieve teamwork performance.

Activity 1. The first idea

Context: "The first idea" is a teambuilding game that encourages quick thinking and creativity in a fun and interactive environment. The purpose of this game is to encourage participants to quickly generate ideas and solutions for different given challenges or problems.

Rules of conduct: Participants are divided into balanced teams so that there is a diversity of perspectives and skills in each team. Teams are told that they will need to quickly generate ideas for different problems or challenges. Game rules and time limits are set for each stage of the game. Each team is given a specific challenge or task to generate ideas. These challenges can be varied and can be related to the team's areas of interest or they can target common problems they face in their work.

Once the teams have received the challenges, the game begins. Each team has a limited time to generate as many ideas as possible related to the given challenge. Participants must quickly come up with as many ideas as possible to solve or address the given challenge. It is important to encourage all team members to contribute and be open to new and innovative ideas. At the end of the brainstorming time, each team presents their ideas. These can be discussed, evaluated, and compared to highlight the most creative and feasible solutions.

An example of this application can be seen in Figure 8.1.

Figure 8.1. The first idea

Benefits of this exercise: "The first idea" game is a great way to stimulate creativity and collaboration within a team. It is an exercise that can be adapted to suit the specific goals and needs of the group and can be useful for developing problem-solving and creative thinking skills. Writing down the first solution that comes to mind can help you find new perspectives and paths.

Activity 2. The napkin list

Context: "The napkin list" is a teambuilding game that encourages communication, planning, and collaboration among team members. This game involves creating a list of simple goals or tasks, which participants must complete using only one or more napkins, divided into smaller pieces.

Rules of conduct: Facilitators divide participants into teams of equal size. Teams must complete a series of tasks using only pieces of tissue paper. These tasks could be diverse and could include building an object, solving a puzzle, making a drawing, or any other simple task. Facilitators will ensure that the teams' tasks are varied and require different approaches to solve.

Each team will start working on the tasks on the list using only the napkins they received. Participants must work together to solve each task on the list. This requires effective communication, planning, and creativity.

As teams succeed in completing each task, it is marked as completed. It is important to monitor progress and provide encouragement to maintain energy and enthusiasm.

Benefits of this exercise: "The napkin list" game is an interactive and fun way to stimulate collaboration and creative thinking within a team. It is an activity that can be adapted to suit the specific teambuilding objectives and can be modified according to the number of participants and the level of difficulty desired.

Activity 3. Personal creation

Context: "The personal creation" teambuilding game encourages participants to use their creativity, collaborative skills, and innovative thinking to create something within a limited amount of time. This game can vary depending on the specific goals of the team and can involve various creative activities such as art, design, construction, problem solving, or even presentations.

Rules of conduct: Establish game goals and provide the team with the resources and materials needed to create something. These can include art and craft materials, paper, pencils, playdough, Legos, or any other activity-specific items, and tools. Divide participants into balanced teams and provide a specific task or project to work on. This can be a problem-solving task, a design project, a creative presentation, or anything else that encourages creativity and collaboration. Teams start working on their projects, planning, and implementing creative ideas. It is important to encourage collaboration and communication between team members to exploit different perspectives and skills.

The time limit is essential in this game to encourage focus and quick decision making. Allocating a specific period for project completion encourages teams to be efficient and manage available resources. At the end of the work period, each team presents or exhibits their creation in front of the other teams. This time can be used to evaluate and appreciate the work done, give feedback, and learn from the experience.

A snapshot of the results of this application can be seen in Figure 8.2.

Figure 8.2. Personal creation.

Benefits of this exercise: "The personal creation" game in a teambuilding is a great way to promote innovative thinking and creativity among team members. It can be tailored to suit the specific goals and needs of the group.

Activity 4. The range of perspectives

Context: The game involves forming teams of 5–15 people, and the game could last 30–60 min.

Rules of conduct: The team members are presented with several topics on which opinions and ideas are desired. Topics are written on a whiteboard, and team members are given paper and pen. Everyone is asked to jot down their thoughts and stick the notes on the board under the topic at hand. The notes are then organized into teams. An attempt will be made to group similar ideas to the left of the subject, and those that stand out will be pasted to the right. This will result in a wide range of common ideas and opinions on the left and original ideas on the right.

Benefits of this exercise: This game is an opportunity to list the team's perspectives on various topics.

Activity 5. What would X do?

Context: The game involves the formation of teams of 5–10 people, and the game could last 45–60 min.

Rules of conduct: The team is presented with a problem, and team members are asked to think of a known person or leader they admire (celebrity, businessman, relative, etc.). The challenge to colleagues is to think about the problem and find a solution as if they were in that person's shoes. An example of this application can be seen in Figure 8.3.

Benefits of this exercise: Thinking without an outside perspective does not always solve a problem efficiently or effectively. Solutions are sometimes easier to find if the person stands in for another person with known problems.

Activity 6. Team tracking

Context: "The team chase" is a teambuilding activity that encourages problem solving along with cooperation, communication, and strategizing in a competitive and fun environment. This game involves dividing participants into teams and following clues or tasks to reach the destination, completing various challenges along the way. The game involves forming teams of 6–24 people, and the game could last 1–3 h.

Rules of conduct: Participants are divided into teams of equal size that can be created according to different criteria, such as skills, experience, or other

Figure 8.3. What would X do?

relevant characteristics. Facilitators will ensure that all participants are aware of the rules of the game and its objectives. The safety rules and playground boundaries are clarified.

Each team is provided with a set of clues or tasks that will guide them throughout the game. These clues can consist of questions, puzzles, navigation directions, or physical or mental challenges. Both teams start at the same time and receive the first set of clues or instructions. Each team must plan their strategy and start solving the clues to progress in the game.

As teams solve tasks or clues, they advance to the next stages of the game. Each stage may bring new challenges or clues leading to the destination.

Benefits of this exercise: "The team chase" game can be adapted to the location and available resources, and can be a fun and interactive way to promote collaboration and team spirit in teambuilding activities. A good team chase game will act as a fun challenge and give everyone a chance to shine and show off their talents. Each team member can play their part in the team's success. This game will create a bond between team members and help them discover new sides of their teammates that are still unknown to them.

Activity 7. The escape game

Context: Playing an escape room as part of a teambuilding involves specific habits and requires close collaboration between team members to solve puzzles and escape from a fictional room or situation within a limited time.

Rules of conduct: Participants are divided into numerically balanced teams with varied abilities. Each team will need to include people who can contribute different types of skills and knowledge. All participants understand the rules and objectives of the game. Participants from each team must work together to solve the puzzles and find the solution that will allow them to escape the room.

Facilitators present a metaphorical scenario as exciting as possible. Each escape room has a theme and a story, for example, it can be prisoners who need to escape from prison, people stuck in a haunted room, etc. Team members are encouraged to work together to solve puzzles and find clues to open doors or uncover hidden treasures. Puzzles can range from secret numbers or codes to hidden words and other riddles.

Benefits of this exercise: Escape rooms in teambuilding are excellent for strengthening relationships between team members, developing teamwork skills, and stimulating creative—creative thinking. Team thinking and active listening are essential for success. Time is limited in an escape room. Teams must manage their time efficiently to solve the puzzles and escape.

Activity 8. The perfect square

Context: "The perfect square" game involves problem-solving focused on setting a collective goal and finding ways to work together to achieve it.

Rules of conduct: Participants are divided into teams of equal size, with each team having a leader or moderator to facilitate the process. Each team is given the task of recreating a "perfect square"—a square of equal size made up of various available objects or materials (e.g., blocks, ribbons, paper, wooden sticks, etc.). Teams must follow certain rules, such as square size, available materials, time allotted, and any other restrictions set.

Each team will start planning and strategizing to build the perfect square. After planning, the teams get to work to build the perfect square using the materials provided. It is important to monitor time and for facilitators to ensure that teams are working effectively to complete the task within the allotted time. At the end of the time, each team presents the constructed square. Moderators or other participants can evaluate each team according to the degree of similarity with the established objective.

A suitable example of a task might be to form a perfect square using a string with the participants' eyes closed. When the team is sure they have created a perfect square, they can let the rope down and open their eyes.

Benefits of this exercise: "The perfect square" game is a fun and interactive activity that emphasizes collaboration, problem solving, and strategic thinking within a team. It is a great way to promote teamwork and encourage participants to find creative and effective solutions together.

Activity 9. Time travel

Context: "Time travel" in teambuilding is an activity that encourages creativity and problem-solving to solve tasks or challenges related to fictional time travel. This game can be adapted in various ways, but the essence remains the same: participants must complete tasks that involve passing through various fictional or real historical periods or events.

Rules of conduct: Facilitators define a story or scenario to serve as the background for time travel. It can be related to travel to different historical periods or locations, or it can be a completely fictional story that requires solving specific tasks to progress the journey. Participants are divided into teams and are explained the story of time travel, as well as the objectives they must complete to progress in the game.

Each stage of time travel may have specific tasks or challenges related to that period or location. These tasks may include solving puzzles, finding hidden clues, interpreting cultural or historical clues, or other specific tasks that must be completed to advance the journey.

Teams are given resources or clues to help them solve tasks. These can be maps, documents, encrypted messages, or other objects that provide the information needed to move on to the next stage of the journey. Each team must manage their time efficiently and progress their journey by solving tasks or challenges within a limited time.

An example of this application can be seen in Figure 8.4.

Benefits of this exercise: The Time Travel game is an engaging way to foster collaboration, creativity, and strategic thinking within the team, allowing participants to engage in an interactive story and work together to solve challenges encountered on their fictional journey through time.

Figure 8.4. Time travel.

The team is stimulated to remember their priorities and create stronger bonds between team members. A divided or stressed team will benefit from sharing personal memories that have nothing to do with work, thus prompting a sense of belonging.

Activity 10. The paper airplane

Context: "The paper airplane" activity emphasizes creativity, collaboration, and competition in a fun and interactive way. This game can vary depending on the rules and objectives set, but the essence of it is to build and test paper airplanes to see which can fly further or more accurately.

Rules of conduct: Participants are divided into teams of equal size. Each team will work together to build paper airplanes and test them in a flying competition. Facilitators explain the rules for paper airplane building and flying competition. Evaluation criteria can be set, such as flight distance, flight duration, or landing accuracy.

Teams are given standard materials for building paper airplanes, such as sheets of paper, paper clips, or glue (depending on the rules set). Each team must collaborate and create the planes that meet the flight criteria. After building the planes, the teams test the planes to see which ones fly farther or more accurately. Organizers can mark the flight distance or evaluate according to pre-set criteria.

Teams test their planes and compete to see who achieves the best result according to set criteria. Organizers can keep track of performances and award points or recognition based on results achieved.

Benefits of this exercise: "The paper airplane" activity is a fun and interactive way to promote solving concrete tasks, using collaboration, creativity, and teamwork skills in a playful and competitive environment.

Activity 11. The tower building

Context: "The tower building" game is about building the tallest tower possible using the materials provided. This game does not require technical knowledge or specific skills but focuses on the team's ability to work together and solve problems in a creative way.

Materials needed: Building materials such as wooden blocks, popsicle sticks, plastic cups or similar items, and a spacious work area.

Rules of conduct: Participants are divided into equal teams. Generally, a team consists of 3–6 people to enable effective collaboration. The objective of the game and the basic rules are explained.

The goal is to build the tallest tower possible using the materials provided. A limited time is set in which the teams must complete the construction of the tower. This can create pressure and encourage rapid collaboration.

Each team receives the necessary materials and begins to build the tower. It is important to encourage communication and collaboration to find the best construction strategies. After the allotted time, the height of each tower is measured. The team that built the tallest tower is declared the winner. Prizes or special recognition may be given to the team that has demonstrated the best collaboration, creativity, or problem-solving skills.

Benefits of this activity: "The tower building" game is a fun and interactive way to improve collaboration and relationships between team members and can be adapted to suit the specific needs and goals of the group involved.

Activity 12. The pancake

Context: "The pancake" game involves team members working together to "twist" and "spin" a "pancake" (generally a large material such as a cloth or paper/cardboard circle) using only a few simple elements, such as ropes or straps. The goal is to spin the "pancake" without it falling or touching the ground.

Materials needed: A "pancake" (a large, light material such as a canvas or a large circle of paper/cardboard) as well as long, strong strings or straps.

Rules of conduct: The participants are divided into equal teams, each team having a few people. It is important to have similar-sized teams to maintain balance and collaboration. The objective of the game and the basic rules are explained.

The goal is to spin the pancake using only strings or belts without falling or touching the ground. A limited time is set in which the teams must plan their strategy and try to spin the "pancake."

Each team must find ways to use the ropes or straps to catch the "pancake" and spin it in the air. Participants must collaborate, coordinate movements, and adapt in real time to keep the "pancake" in the air. The performance of the teams is evaluated according to their ability to rotate the "pancake" and maintain its balance. The team that manages to perform this task in the most successful way is declared the winner. Awards may be given based on criteria such as creativity, collaboration, or demonstrated poise.

Benefits of this activity: Participants must communicate effectively and coordinate movements to rotate the "pancake" without falling. Participants learn to find creative solutions and adapt to changes in real time to achieve the game goal. The game is fun and interactive, which helps build relationships and team spirit. The activity can be adapted according to the number of participants and the specific goals of the teambuilding session.

Activity 13. The remark

Context: The activity aims to develop memory, delve into details, and develop the ability to innovate to compensate for missing information.

Rules of conduct: Create a structure from Lego pieces and hide it in a separate room. The team is divided into groups of two to four people, and each team is given enough Lego pieces to reproduce the structure in not more than 30 min. One player from each team is allowed to look at the original structure for 15 s, then return to their team to describe it. Each team member takes turns looking at the model, the goal being that everyone has had a chance to see it during the game. The first team to reproduce the structure exactly (or almost exactly) wins.

Benefits of this exercise: The team will need to focus on teamwork and communication. Since only one person at a time can see the original, team members will likely be able to observe and describe different constructive elements. The more complex the structure, the more difficult the game will be.

Activity 14. The shipwrecked

Context: The participants are put in the position of shipwrecked people and must collaborate to make strategic choices for their survival.

Rules of conduct: Participants are divided into teams of equal size. Teams may vary depending on the number of participants and the complexity of the shipwreck simulation. A fictional shipwreck scenario is created. This may include details of the castaways' plight, the limited resources they have at their disposal, and the specific challenges they face.

Participants are given limited resources (symbolized by imaginary objects or resources such as water, food, building materials, etc.) and must prioritize and manage these resources to survive. Resources, such as water bottles, matches, food, etc. are placed in the "shipwreck area." One can also print the images on the cards to make the task easier. Each item should be in limited quantity, some being rarer than others (e.g., more water than food, less tarps than teams, more knives than ropes, etc.).

Participants must identify and solve various problems and challenges to survive. These can include building a shelter, finding food, purifying water, etc. Teams must collaborate and find creative solutions to meet challenges.

Benefits of this exercise: Participants are exposed to decision-making under pressure and managing limited resources, which helps them develop strategic thinking skills and adaptability. Surviving in a difficult situation builds trust and team spirit between participants, stimulating collaboration and mutual support.

The game teaches participants to effectively manage resources and identify priorities during a crisis. This game will test problem-solving skills, encourage collaboration, and allow the team to show their leadership skills. In general, teams with the best leaders do best when it comes to making quick decisions.

Activity 15. The team flag

Context: "The team flag" activity is a game that stimulates creativity, cooperation, and the manifestation of aesthetic skills.

Rules of conduct: The team is divided into groups of two to four people, and each group receives paper and pens. Each group must design an emblem or flag to represent the group. After everyone has put the finishing touches on the drawings, a general presentation is organized where each group explains how they arrived at that image. This exercise will also be an opportunity to discuss how each group identified common values and coordinated throughout the creative process.

Benefits of this exercise: The image of each group represents their collective identity; it encourages working together to achieve the project.

Activity 16. The sale

Context: "The sale" game is a teambuilding exercise that aims to improve communication, negotiation, and collaboration skills in a team. This game involves simulating a sales and negotiation situation in a controlled and fun environment.

Rules of conduct: Participants are divided into teams of three or four, depending on the size of the group. Each team will be given a sales scenario or a fictitious product to sell. This could be an imaginary object, a service, or anything else that requires a persuasive presentation and argument to be sold.

Teams will have a limited amount of time to prepare a presentation or sales pitch to buy assigned to them. This preparation can involve the stability of a sales speech, the identification of product advantages, the creation of negotiation strategies, etc. Each team will present their product and try to sell it to the other teams (or "buyers"). The goal is to be as convincing and persuasive as possible to get an imaginative sale of their product.

Benefits of this exercise: Through this game, participants can practice their communication, negotiation, strategic thinking, and collaboration skills in a safe and fun environment. It is also a great way to emphasize the importance of interpersonal skills and teamwork in a sales and business relationship context. If a team does not already work in marketing or sales, playing the game is an opportunity to see things from a different perspective.

Activity 17. The business puzzle

Context: "The business puzzle" game is a teambuilding exercise designed to promote collaboration, communication, and strategy in a team. This game involves solving a physical puzzle, with multiple pieces, but with a specific approach that requires the involvement and coordination of all team members.

Rules of conduct: The team is divided into smaller groups, each group having the responsibility of solving a part of the puzzle. Each part of the puzzle can be distributed according to its complexity or how the pieces are interconnected. The pieces of the puzzle are distributed equally among the small teams, without them having a global picture of the final puzzle.

Teams must collaborate and communicate effectively to solve the puzzle. Although each team works on a separate part, they must coordinate their efforts to ensure that all the pieces fit together in the end. As each group solves their part of the puzzle, they must work together to fully assemble the puzzle and form the final image or pattern.

Benefits of this exercise: "The business puzzle" game not only strengthens the bonds between team members but also emphasizes the importance of strategic planning, effective communication, and collaboration in achieving a common goal. It gives participants an interactive and fun insight into how the team can work together to solve problems and achieve success in everyday work activities.

Activity 18. The globe

Context: "The globe" activity is a teambuilding exercise that involves collaboration and communication within a team to achieve a common goal. This game aims to encourage collaboration, planning, and coordination in an interactive and fun way.

Rules of conduct: Participants are divided into smaller teams, each team being responsible for decorating a portion of a giant globe or world map. Each team is given a specific region or country that they must decorate on the globe. This may involve the use of colors, symbols, images, or messages to illustrate distinctive or cultural features of that region.

Teams work together to decide how to decorate and represent their assigned region or country on the globe as authentically and creatively as possible. At the end, all teams bring together the decorated portions of the globe and assemble them to create the complete picture of the world. This stage requires coordination and collaboration to ensure that each piece fits correctly and blends with the others.

Benefits of this exercise: "The globe" activity is an interactive and fun activity that encourages team spirit, trust, and collaboration to achieve a common goal. This game can highlight the importance of teamwork and coordination in a collaborative and interactive work environment.

Activity 19. The treasure hunt

Context: Treasure hunting is an interactive and fun teambuilding activity that involves solving clues and finding specific objects or places in a predetermined environment. The goal is to encourage collaboration, communication, and creative thinking among participants within a team.

Rules of conduct: Facilitators define the area where the treasure hunt will take place and set the goals and rules of the game. Clues or tracks are also created that will guide participants to hidden treasures or targets to find. Treasures can take the form of a list of photos to be taken (e.g., a red object, a photo of all colleagues, the CEO's car, etc.), or objects to be collected (e.g., the company brochure, a yellow signature sticker ticket the manager, a bag of ketchup from the cafeteria, etc.) or other activities that must be carried out along a well-defined route.

Participants are divided into smaller teams, each with a few members. These teams will compete to find the hidden treasures. Each team is given the first clue or clue to lead them to the next location or objective. These clues can be written clues, GPS coordinates, encrypted messages, or any other instructions to help them advance in their hunt. Teams can work together or separately to interpret clues and find the next location or objective. At each location discovered, they will find a new clue to guide them further. The ultimate objective is to find the treasure or complete the treasure hunt within a predetermined time.

Benefits of this exercise: A teambuilding treasure hunt is a great way to promote team spirit, collaboration, strategic thinking, and problem-solving in a fun and interactive environment. It is also a perfect opportunity to build bonds between team members and highlight the importance of communication and collaboration in achieving a common goal.

Activity 20. The falling egg

Context: "The falling egg" activity is a teambuilding exercise that emphasizes creativity, planning, and problem-solving skills within a team. This exercise involves building a structure to protect an egg from breaking when it is dropped from a certain height.

Rules of conduct: Participants are given limited materials such as paper, scotch tape, bamboo sticks, playdough, or anything else available to use to build a structure to protect an egg. Rules are set for how high the egg will fall and how the built structure will be evaluated. Participants usually have a limited amount of time to plan and build their egg protector.

Teams work together to design and build a structure that can protect an egg when it is dropped from a specified height. The egg is placed in each structure, and each team tests their device. The egg is then allowed to fall from the set height.

Benefits of this exercise: This activity not only encourages collaboration and creativity, but also develops skills such as planning, problem solving and adaptability in the face of challenges. It also provides an opportunity to discuss the importance of teamwork and learn lessons for improving collaboration in the future.

Activity 21. The right price

Context: "The right price" is a teambuilding activity that relies on negotiation, decision-making and communication skills of the participants. This activity involves simulating a buying and selling situation, where participants must set prices and reach an agreement to complete a transaction.

Rules of conduct: Participants are divided into teams and given a fixed amount of fictitious "money" or resources, which they must use to purchase various items or services. Organizers present participants with a series of items or services (fictional or real) that are available for purchase. They can have different values and distinct characteristics.

Teams start negotiating with other teams to buy or sell the presented items/services. The goal is to set favorable prices for them and get the best deals.

Benefits of this exercise: "The right price" is an interactive and engaging activity that emphasizes negotiation, collaboration, and strategic thinking skills, giving participants the opportunity to apply these skills in a controlled and fun environment.

Activity 22. The code of conduct

Context: "The code of conduct" activity in teambuilding is a way for team members to collaborate to create a set of rules, norms, and values that govern behavior and interactions within the group or organization. This activity is designed to encourage communication, collaboration, and the definition of a common set of principles that will improve the organizational climate and relationships between colleagues.

Rules of conduct: Participants are divided into teams and asked to discuss and identify the core values, norms, and principles they wish to promote and uphold within their organization or team. Teams begin to brainstorm and discuss the values they believe are essential for effective collaboration and a positive work environment. These can include loyalty, respect, integrity, transparency, diversity, team spirit, etc.

Based on the discussions and ideas generated, each team works to formulate a set of rules and principles that reflect the values and norms identified. These are drafted in the form of a "Code of Conduct" or "Book of Values" that will guide behavior and interactions within the team or organization. Each team presents the code of conduct created to the other teams or to the whole group. A discussion is opened to evaluate and make possible adjustments or additions to reach a consensus.

After the discussions and possible changes are completed, the code of conduct is officially adopted and promoted within the organization. It becomes an important tool for guiding behavior and relationships between team members or colleagues within the organization.

Benefits of this exercise: This activity not only facilitates the development of a common set of values and rules but also strengthens cohesion and understanding among team members. In addition, it promotes a healthy organizational culture and a harmonious work environment based on mutual respect and collaboration.

Bibliography

Baldwin, T. T., Boomer, W. H. & Rubin, R. S. (2008). *Developing Management Skills: What Great Managers Know and Do*. Boston: McGraw-Hill.

Colonna, C.-H. (2017). Le «team building», solution miracle ou miroir aux alouettes ? in Les Echos. <https://www.lesechos.fr/idees-debats/cercle/le-team-building-solution-miracle-ou-miroir-aux-alouettes-1011474>.

Kauffman, D. (2015). *L'équipe en crise, in* Les Cahiers Internationaux de Psychologie Sociale L, (Numéro 106) 2. Éditions Presses universitaires de Liège.

Klein, C., DiazGranados, D., Salas, E., Le, H., Burke, C. S., Lyons, R., & Goodwin, G. F. (2009). « Does Team Building Work? » *Small Group Research 40*(2).

Moine, J.-F. & Colombo, J. (2002). *Communiquer en Situation de Crise*. ESF Editeur – CEGOS

Schein, E. H. (1969). *Process Consultation: Its Role in Organization Development*. Reading, MA: Addison-Wesley.

Schein, E. H. (1999). *Process Consultation Revisited: Building the Helping Relationship*. Reading, MA: Addison-Wesley.

Sweeney, P. D., & McFarlin, D. B. (2002). *Organizational Behavior: Solutions for Management*. McGraw-Hill.

*** *Comment evaluer l'efficacite du team building au sein de votre entreprise?* In Gothman City Gazette <https://batman-escape.com/article/team-building-efficace-comment-mesurer-son-impact-au-sein-entreprise>

CHAPTER 9

Feedback and reflection activities

Daniel Roşu, Andreea Laura Bădulescu, and Manuela Mihaela Ciucurel

Summary: Feedback and reflection activities in teambuilding are essential and structured processes that allow participants to examine their experiences, share their observations, and improve their individual and team skills. The purpose of carrying out this stage of teambuilding is for the participants to give and receive constructive information to improve team performance and transfer it to the professional environment. This is a two-way communication process and involves careful analysis and evaluation of the experiences lived within the activities. Participants are encouraged to examine their thoughts, feelings, and actions, identify what they have learned and how they can apply these learnings to their personal or professional lives. Reflection helps them develop their capacity for self-analysis and better understand their own reactions and behaviors. The open and respectful framework ensures the efficiency of the various techniques for completing this stage. The stage usually excludes movement and takes place based on dialogue between the participating members, stimulated constructively by the facilitators.

Keywords: Deciphering experience, performance evaluation, appreciation, analysis of causes, effects in professional activity.

Feedback and reflection activities in teambuilding are exercises and interactions planned to facilitate the process of giving and receiving constructive feedback among team members (Roşu, 2008, 2015). These activities encourage members to express their thoughts and feelings openly and learn from their experiences to improve collaboration and collective performance.

Reflect involves the action of thinking deeply, meditating, and pondering, which draws attention to some fundamental procedural components: thinking, affectivity, and availability (intention). Also, reflecting requires an optimal context that predisposes to a specific state associated with a high capacity for presence, awareness, and the intention to provide time and space for the analysis of a thought, or a lived or anticipated situation, with the aim of a detailed understanding, of complexity.

9.1. The importance of feedback and reflection activities in the context of teambuilding

Simon Priest, referring to corporate actions, links them to experiential learning. This, in the view of the mentioned author, is based more on active action, rather than on passive action. That way, people practice the skills they learn and are more likely to maintain their change at work. Experiential learning becomes "experiential" when elements of reflection, transfer, and support are added to the core experience.

It thus becomes important to explain the meaning of the three mentioned concepts:

- Reflection—referring to the deliberate examination of the process of an experience, which can enhance awareness of learning and lead to changes in feeling, thinking or behavior arising from that experience.
- Transfer—with reference to the change obtained following the running of an experiential program; this change must occur in the real-life workplace.
- Support—referring to providing time, resources, and team or project opportunities to enable people to continue change (or initiate new learning), thus also reducing their resistance to change.

As Priest points out, the term *facilitation* is more appropriate than *reflection* since reflection is the key to deep learning (the one that leads to lasting change), it must be facilitated, during or after an experience. He also shows that four facilitation techniques have special relevance for experiential programs:

- Funnelling—using sequenced questions during or after an experience to guide debriefing.
- Frontloading—using punctuated questions before or during an experience to redirect reflection.
- Framing—introducing the experience in a manner that enhances its relevance and meaning.
- Solution-focused—changing the focus of questions away from problems or dysfunctions.

The transfer of learning and change from experiential programs to real life is often a critical concept in facilitation, being most often a difficult outcome to achieve. Since many of the characteristics of experiential programs compared to real-life situations are very different, it is very difficult for the participants in teambuilding to create transfer what they learned in the work activity.

Thus, as a result of the activities undertaken and the completion of the reflection stage, the *transfer* is expected to take place, which can be of the following types:

- *Specific transfer:* what was learned in teambuilding is directly transferred to the workplace. For example, in teambuilding, a new method of promoting a product was learned, and this is similarly transposed by the participant to the workplace. So, the learning product from teambuilding is used in a similar way in the workplace.
- *Non-specific transfer:* with reference to general behaviors learned in order to apply them in different situations. In this situation, there is a big gap between the learning environment and the application environment. For example, mastering a new way of solving problems, learned in teambuilding, is applied with difficulty in the workplace.
- *Metaphorical transfer:* applied in an attempt to reduce the gap between the learning environment and the workplace; for this purpose, metaphorical applications are used in teambuilding, apparently different from real-life situations. A metaphor is an idea, object, or description used in place of another different idea, object, or description, to achieve a comparative similarity or similitude between the two. By understanding and embracing the metaphor, teambuilding participants can associate learning environments with workplace application environments.

Today's society, dominated by technological evolution and the fast pace in which various experiences follow one another, inevitably leads to the acceleration of the way people relate to themselves, to others, and to life in general (Rosu & Miroiu, 2018). From here, it could derive obvious negative repercussions in terms of psycho-physical health, respectively at the level of psycho-personal well-being, with effects on all other components of man (cognitive, organic, and spiritual), in all areas of life: personal, family, social, and professional.

From the psychological studies carried out in the business sector, a series of benefits are extracted from the techniques of providing feedback/mirroring, with the condition that this communication is of an empathetic type. Among the advantages of *empathic listening*, we can list:

- *Can build trust*—Empathic listening is an active listening technique that requires attention to the person's non-verbal cues, and the ability to "read between the lines" to understand what the other person is really thinking and feeling. By feeling understood, the employee participates in increasing self-confidence, making it essential for leaders to trust their teams, as this increases employee productivity and engagement.
- *Optimizes problem-solving*—Through empathic listening, one can get to the heart of the problem. A complex understanding of the situation (rational and empathetic) could help to clarify the real problem, and attention to key details participating in identifying the most suitable solution.
- *Selects the optimal decisions*—Leaders often underestimate the contributions and opinions of employees, knowing that the others' perspective could help to understand things that otherwise could not be considered.
- *Realizes team cohesion*—Creating a work environment where employees feel seen and heard could participate in building greater team coherence, empathic listening participating in shaping an organizational culture based on trust and cooperation.
- *Strengthens employee wellness*—When employees feel seen and understood by their superiors, they may perceive wellness at a higher level. This can help reduce the risk of employee burnout, reduce stress, and employee turnover. Well-being, in a psycho-physical sense, will help to obtain better results at work, implicitly achieving work objectives, effectively and efficiently.
- *Optimizes organizational productivity*—When team members are happy, they are more productive, minimizing the risk of employee burnout, implicit absenteeism, or loss of interest in work tasks.
- *Minimizes conflict situations*—In a conflict situation, at least one of the parties feels misunderstood (often, it's both). Empathetic listening to conflicting parties is one of the best ways to defuse tensions. The person who directly feels the state of conflict can consciously practice giving up their own arguments and focusing on the other's arguments to increase clarity on the source of the conflict and identify the optimal solutions to resolve the situation.

A Eurobarometer survey conducted in June 2023 showed that almost 1 in 2 people (46% of the EU population) have experienced emotional or psychosocial problems, such as feeling depressed/anxious, in the past 12 months. Mental health must be understood as an extremely sensitive and important subject, which needs to be approached very carefully in the organizational culture. Mental health is an integral part of human health, being essential for a resilient society, for a productive economy. Based on this argument, we can consider that in the contemporary stage, the objective process of feedback and reflection in teambuilding can be strongly influenced by this situation!

Beyond the immediate specific benefits of mental health, this phenomenon can be understood more widely in the form of a domino system, in which one stage can determine the other, the balance built today, determining the one tomorrow.

Mental health refers to physical, psychological, and social well-being. For example, depression increases the risk of many types of physical health problems, especially long-term conditions such as diabetes, heart disease, and stroke. Similarly, the presence of chronic conditions can increase the risk of mental illness (*Chronic Illness and Mental Health Recognizing and Treating Depression*, National Institute of Mental Health, 2021).

Mental health affects the way people think, feel and act, participating in determining how people manage stress, influence relationships with others, and determine decision-making.

Amid these existential challenges, the quality of decisions could counterbalance the number of resources consumed (in the psycho-physical sense) to face the challenges. The ability to "deal" with various situations is called "resilience."

Resilience does not only mean the absence of disease but also is a dynamic process that allows the individual to successfully adapt to various situations perceived as negative throughout life. The three fundamental pillars of resilience are (Rutten et al., 2013):

- Emotionally secure relationships (in the family, in society, in a professional context).
- Experiencing positive emotions (at the level of optimistic attitude/thinking).
- Finding and following a purpose in life (giving a direction to one's own existence).

Feedback and reflection directly support personal development, this need for reflection and reflective behavior is of particular importance in work teams, both of which require reflective skills on the part of participants (Schley, 2014).

The concept of "*personal development*" can be understood from several perspectives (physical, mental, personal, or professional) but in general, the common denominator of personal development refers to the qualitative and quantitative leap that a person can make at a given moment of his life (Reisinger & Turner, 2003). Personal development can be understood as an experiential process (a life experience) that involves the discovery of personal resources and their fulfillment, to optimize the quality of personal life. The positive effects in terms of personal optimization will be able to create effects beyond one's own person (Petrick, 2004), participating in increasing the quality of relationships with others, and motivational optimization in all sectors of life.

Personal development is a process that involves a series of factors that can be likened to the pieces of a puzzle that can make up a final result in the form of a harmonious, meaningful image. This process could enable understanding of the past and determining clear directions for the present or future stages of life.

The experience of personal development requires time, motivation, commitment, and trust (Rosu, 2019). In this process, various obstacles will be encountered, but each path, longer or shorter, begins with the first step, which determines the next, becoming vital to preserving energy, active interest and availability for health and psycho-physical balance.

The process of *personal development* can be achieved in two big stages:

- *The first level* is a very personal one and concerns the relationship with oneself, the identification of personal sources and resources, the clarification of personal objectives, the crystallization of self-identity, and the polishing of personality traits in the sense of personal optimization. Through reflection, this level can be easily traversed.
- *The second level* involves self-information that can make the transition from "me" to "others," understanding self-becoming from a perspective that no longer focuses on very personal aspects but on "me in and through the world." Through reflection and feedback, this process can be optimized.

Personal unity, balance, enthusiasm, motivation and energy, path and meaning take shape in the first level and are maximized in the second level, which makes the transition from "self" to "world."

Beyond the personal benefit—the relationship with oneself, personal development participates in the re-signification of one's own life experiences, and new perspectives for the interpretation of previously lived situations and relationships. Changing perspective could help to reorganize one's own living context and relationships with others, with direct benefits on all levels of life.

The process of personal development involves not only self-analysis but also concrete actions. Thus, only personal analysis (state of reflection) will not be enough, it would be equally important to act in the direction of implementing new attitudes and behaviors through which to build new resources and personal skills.

The entire process of personal development and all the implicit benefits will require the ability to be aware of personal needs, objective assessment of the life context, and the availability (desire) for personal optimization.

For all this, the skills to reflect on one's own experience and to reflect on the experience of others will be essential tools:

- *Reflection:* refers to the action of thinking, and meditating (analyzing one's own thoughts).
- *Reflect:* the act of "mirroring" (making an observation about someone or something).

Both forms of action are equally important in the process of personal optimization, whether it refers to the improvement of the relationship with oneself and one's own experiences, or whether the improvement of relations with others is considered (the working group).

Facilitating discussions or deciphering the experience after any activity becomes a very specific thing for teambuilding. Adventure activities or extreme sports are among all the types of activities that allow the participants to make the connection between their lived experiences and the challenges or situations they may encounter in the professional environment. In these situations, the identification of parallels and transferable learning can be particularly useful in the professional reorientation-redirection process.

A reflection sequence at the end of a mountain activity can be seen in Figure 9.1.

Figure 9.1. Reflection after a mountain activity.

9.2. Types of feedback and reflection activities

The following types of activities are used for feedback and reflection:

- Structured feedback sessions: These activities involve moments dedicated to providing feedback in an organized and constructive way. Each team member can give and receive feedback on the performance and contribution of others.
- Post-Activity Discussions: After completing a team activity, members come together to discuss their experience, what went well, and what could be improved. These discussions can help identify lessons learned and possible improvements for the future.
- Self-reflection sessions: These involve moments where each team member can reflect on their own actions, skills, and contributions within the team. The goal is to identify the strengths of your own

behavior and the aspects you can improve. Providing adequate feedback requires objectivity, a process of personal analysis of one's own characteristics, needs and interests, and the correct evaluation of the relationship with oneself, namely the degree of personal satisfaction. All this is to minimize the probability that personal shortcomings interfere with the ability to provide constructive feedback.

- Feedback role plays: These activities involve exercises where team members play specific roles to simulate feedback situations. This can help develop the skills of giving and receiving feedback in an effective way.
- Performance review sessions: These activities may involve the collective evaluation of the team's performance in the context of a specific project or activity. The aim is to identify strengths and areas for improvement.
- Exercises to identify personal and team goals: These involve times when team members express their personal and collective goals and discuss how they can work together to achieve them (Roşu et al. 2022).
- Communication skills development sessions: These activities focus on improving communication skills, active listening and expressing ideas within the team. Socio-emotional skills are essential in the workplace for creating and maintaining good interpersonal relationships. Organizations devote considerable resources to programs designed to improve employees' social and interpersonal skills (Reggio et. all, 2020). Socio-emotional skills rely heavily on assertiveness. This concept characterizes the ability to express one's own experience (sensory-perceptive, cognitive, affective, needs) with empathy for those around. It is based on the ability to be self-aware (perceptions, thoughts, affective experiences, needs), and to express internal experience in a way that is easily understood by others. Assertiveness is an important skill required for successful human interaction. The specialized literature indicates the need to include in the educational process some specially developed programs for the development of assertive behavior (Stoykov, 2020).
- Recognition and Appreciation Sessions: These are times when team members express their gratitude and appreciation for the contributions and efforts of their colleagues (Williams & Soutar, 2009).

These activities are essential to foster an open work environment where members feel comfortable giving and receiving feedback in a constructive way. They contribute to the development of a culture of continuous learning and constant improvement within the team.

9.3. Examples of feedback and reflection activities

These activities encourage reflection and open dialogue between team members, contributing to personal development and improving collaboration and collective performance. They should be conducted in a safe and respectful environment so that a space is created where members feel comfortable sharing and receiving feedback in a constructive way. The importance of feedback has also been confirmed by studies showing that people remember group discussions better, learning in working teams promotes understanding, and there is a tendency to learn more of what is taught and retain it better than when the material is presented in other teaching formats (Barkley, Cross & Major, 2005; Davis, 1993).

As examples of feedback and reflection activities, we mention:

Activity 1. 360-degree feedback session

Context: Team members give and receive feedback to each other about each other's skills, behavior, and contributions to the team.

Rules of conduct: Teambuilding 360-degree feedback sessions is an effective way to gain multiple perspectives on the performance and behavior of each team member. These sessions involve gathering feedback from various peers, superiors, subordinates, and others relevant to each participant. In general, 360-degree feedback sessions in a teambuilding program are carried out like this:

- Selection of participants: A group of evaluators is chosen, which may include team members, colleagues from other departments, superiors, subordinates, or others who have interacted with the participant in a way relevant to the evaluation.
- Establishing evaluation criteria: Establishing the specific criteria that evaluators must follow when evaluating the behavior and performance

of participants. These criteria can be related to specific skills, leadership qualities, communication skills, etc.
- Distribution of questionnaires or feedback forms: Questionnaires or feedback forms are distributed to evaluators. These documents may include open-ended questions or rating scales, as well as spaces for comments and suggestions.
- Confidentiality and anonymity: It is important to ensure that participant feedback will be treated confidentially and that responses will be anonymous to encourage honesty and openness.
- Collection and centralization of feedback: After the evaluators complete the questionnaires or feedback forms, they are collected and centralized by the organizers of the teambuilding program.
- Individual feedback sessions: Participants are provided with the collected feedback in report form, without revealing the identity of the evaluators. Organizers can help interpret feedback and identify strengths and areas for improvement.
- Discussion and action sessions: Participants can discuss the feedback received and identify concrete steps to improve certain aspects of their behavior and performance.
- Personalized Development Plans: Participants can create personalized development plans, where they set specific goals and identify the resources and support needed to achieve those goals.

It is important that 360-degree feedback sessions are conducted with respect, openness, and professionalism. The goal is to provide team members with the opportunity to gain diverse perspectives to develop and contribute to the team's performance as a whole.

Activity 2: Circle of appreciation

Context: Team members sit in a circle and each participant says a positive aspect or achievement of another team member, promoting appreciation and recognition.

Rules of conduct: The appreciation circle in teambuilding is an activity that encourages team members to express gratitude and appreciation to each other. This takes place in an organized and respectful setting, where each participant can share positive thoughts and appreciation with other team members. An appreciation circle in a teambuilding program is held after the following sequence:

- Establishing a framework of respect and confidentiality: Organizers establish a safe and comfortable environment in which team members can express themselves openly and honestly. It is important to ensure confidentiality and promote mutual respect.
- Explaining objectives and rules: Organizers explain the purpose of the activity, which is to provide positive feedback and mutual appreciation. Simple rules can also be set, such as expecting each participant to speak respectfully and listen carefully.
- Circle formation: Participants sit in a circle so they can see and hear each other. It is important to create an environment where everyone feels comfortable participating.
- Circle rotation and mutual appreciation: Each participant chooses a colleague from the circle and expresses their appreciation in a sincere and genuine way. Traits, skills, contributions, or any other positive aspect of that person can be appreciated.
- Time limitation: To ensure that all participants can receive appreciation, the time allotted to each participant can be limited. For example, each person may have 2–3 minutes to express their appreciation.
- Continued rotation: Participants rotate in a circle to continue expressing appreciation to different peers. This process can continue until every team member has had an opportunity to participate.
- Reciprocal receptivity and thanks: The person receiving appreciation responds respectfully, may offer recognition and thanks for kind words.
- Discussion and reflection sessions: After the activity is over, a team discussion and reflection session can be held to share feelings and observations about the experience.

The importance of this activity: The Appreciation Circle is a powerful way to build bonds and strengthen team spirit. It gives team members the opportunity to feel valued and appreciated for their contributions, which can significantly improve team morale and cohesion.

Activity 3: Reflecting on personal and team goals

Context: Each member expresses their personal and collective goals and then discusses how they can be supported and achieved.

Rules of conduct: Reflecting on personal and team goals in teambuilding involves a series of steps designed to help team members clarify their individual goals and integrate them into the team's collective goals. This activity can be done like this:

- Introduction and explanation of purpose: The organizer begins by explaining the purpose of the reflection session. This can be to develop a shared understanding of personal and team goals to ensure everyone is working together in the right direction.
- Request for individual thoughts and wishes: Team members are encouraged to express their personal thoughts and wishes regarding professional development, achievements, and directions in which they wish to progress.
- Clarification of personal goals: Each team member takes the floor and shares his personal goals. These can be related to developing skills, getting promotions or any other aspect important to everyone.
- Connection to team goals: After each member has expressed their personal goals, a discussion is held about how they can fit into the team's goals and priorities. It looks for synergies and ways in which individual goals can contribute to collective success.
- Setting common goals: The team identifies and sets common goals they want to achieve. These can be related to specific projects, improving performance, or achieving a certain level of excellence in certain areas.
- Creation of an action plan: After setting goals, the team can create an action plan that includes the steps needed to achieve those goals. Each member can contribute ideas and suggestions.
- Delegation of responsibilities: It can be established who will be responsible for each stage of the action plan and how members will work together to achieve the set goals.
- Monitoring and reviewing progress: The team can establish ways to monitor progress towards goals and make periodic reviews to ensure they are staying on track.

The importance of this activity: This activity encourages open communication, clarification of expectations, and alignment of individual goals with those of the team. Reflecting on personal and team goals can contribute to better understanding and collaboration within the team.

Activity 4: The letter from the future

Context: Team members write letters to themselves, from the perspective of the future, reflecting on their achievements and how they contributed to the team's success.

Rules of conduct: The future letter in teambuilding is an activity that encourages participants to think about their long-term goals and imagine their future success. This activity is carried out as follows:

- Introduction and explanations: The organizer starts by explaining the purpose and benefits of the exercise. Participants are asked to imagine that they have already achieved all their goals and write a letter to their future selves.
- Defining long-term goals: Participants are asked to reflect on their long-term personal and professional goals. These can be related to career, personal development, relationships, health, etc.
- Instructions for writing the letter: Participants are given clear instructions on how to write the letter. They should address themselves from the future as if they have already achieved the set goals.
- Key elements of the letter: The letter may include the following elements:
  - Acknowledgment of achievements: Participants express gratitude for their own work and dedication that helped them achieve their goals.
  - Description of the objectives achieved: Write in detail the objectives that were achieved and how they contributed to the overall success.
  - Feelings and emotions associated with achievements: Participants express their feelings, emotions and feelings related to their achievements. It can include moments of pride, happiness, satisfaction, etc.
- Ending the letter with thoughts of encouragement: Participants write the end of their letter with thoughts of encouragement and motivation for themselves in the future.

- Sealing and keeping the letter: After the letter is written, each participant seals it in an envelope and keeps it for themselves or gives it to the organizer for safekeeping until they are opened.
- Reflection and sharing session (optional): After writing the letters, participants can be encouraged to share their thoughts or feelings with the rest of the team if they wish to do so.

The importance of this activity: This activity is a powerful way to help participants clarify their long-term goals and envision success. The letter from the future can also serve as a source of inspiration and motivation to work with determination toward achieving these goals. It is important that participants feel safe and comfortable sharing their thoughts in this activity.

Activity 5: Small group reflection sessions

Context: The team breaks into small groups and discusses recent experiences or how they can improve collaboration and collective performance.

Rules of conduct: Small group reflection sessions in teambuilding are an effective way to facilitate open and constructive discussions between team members. These sessions provide an opportunity to share thoughts, experiences, and observations in a more intimate and focused setting. Such a session proceeds as follows:

- *Small group selection*: The organizer divides team members into small groups, either based on common interests, roles, or projects they worked on together.
- *Establishing a safe and respectful environment*: The organizer ensures an environment where team members feel comfortable sharing thoughts and providing open and constructive feedback.
- *Defining the objectives of the session*: The organizer explains the purpose of the reflection session, which can be, for example, to analyze recent experiences, identify lessons learned or develop strategies for improvement.
- *Guiding questions or discussion topics*: The organizer can provide specific questions or topics to guide the small group discussion. These can be related to team performance, communication, collaboration, problem-solving, etc.

- *Discussion rotation*: Team members can share their thoughts, experiences and observations. Each participant has an opportunity to speak and the others listen carefully.
- *Constructive feedback and active listening*: Team members are encouraged to provide feedback in a constructive and respectful manner. Also, each participant must listen carefully and respect the opinions of others.
- *Identify lessons learned and areas for improvement*: Participants discuss what they have learned from the experience and identify areas that can be improved in the future.
- *Concluding the session with a summary and action plan*: The facilitator concludes the session with a summary of the main points discussed and encourages team members to identify concrete steps they will take as a result of this reflection.

Activity 6: Personal Reflection Journal

Context: Each member keeps a journal in which they record thoughts, feelings, and observations about their own performance and interactions within the team.

The personal reflection journal can support the process of self-knowledge and self-overcoming (Koziol, 2021) with the aim of personal optimization, aspects that fundamentally participate in reaching and maintaining a higher goal, such as resilience. *Clarification of self-related thoughts* can be done using self-questioning such as: "*It starts with understanding that no one can make you feel inferior against your will. What do you think this could mean for you?*"; "*Build a healthy image by taking small steps. Where do you think you could start?*"; "*Smile at yourself, encourage yourself, compliment yourself. How often do you do this? How easy is it for you?*"; "*Make a list of your positive traits, skills you're proud of, and achievements you consider successful. How fast could you build it?*"; "*Avoid things and people who discourage and demoralize you or behave in ways that make you uncomfortable. Are you already thinking about someone/something in particular?*"; "*Look yourself and others in the eye. How easy is it for you to do that?*"

Self-analysis implies a high reflective capacity, which can be accessed against the background of a state of relaxation/relaxation and concentration on the well-defined objective: personal optimization. The process of self-analysis does not imply a radical change regarding the specific, defining elements of the person (personality structure, descriptive thoughts, or behaviors), but it is important that the person is available for self-observation, that is, the identification of aspects that can be evaluated as blocking factors in relation to others, with the aim of optimizing personal and social skills.

Rules of conduct: A teambuilding personal reflection journal is an activity in which participants record their thoughts, feelings, observations, and personal reflections about the experiences and activities of the teambuilding program. The activity goes like this:

- *Distribution of journals and explanations*: The organizer provides each participant with a journal or a notebook in which they will record their personal reflections. It is important to explain the purpose and benefits of this activity.
- *Establish a reflection schedule*: Participants are encouraged to set aside time to reflect on experiences, depending on the teambuilding schedule. This can be done every evening after the activities are over or at dedicated times.
- *Encouraging honesty and authenticity*: Participants are encouraged to be honest and authentic in their entries. It is important that they express their thoughts and feelings in an open and honest way.
- *Reflection guidance*: The organizer can provide guides or questions to guide the participants' reflections. These questions can be related to activities, experiences, personal discoveries, lessons learned, goals achieved, etc.
- *Promotion of self-knowledge and personal development*: Participants are encouraged to think about how teambuilding experiences can help them to know themselves better and develop in different aspects.
- *Revisiting Past Reflections*: During the teambuilding program, participants can revisit past reflections to note evolution and changes in thinking and feelings.
- *Sharing option (optional)*: Participants can have the option to share with other team members certain aspects of their reflection journal if they feel comfortable doing so.
- *Group reflection session*: A group reflection session can be held at the end of the program, where participants can share their experiences and discuss lessons learned.

The importance of this activity: A personal reflection journal gives participants a way to process their experiences and learn from them. This activity can contribute to personal development and to the consolidation of the learning within the teambuilding program. It is important to respect the confidentiality of personal reflections and to create a safe environment where participants feel comfortable sharing their thoughts.

Activity 7: Cause and effect analysis sessions

Context: Team members discuss recent problems or successes and try to identify the causes that led to these results and what can be improved.

Rules of conduct: Cause and effect analysis sessions in teambuilding are an effective way to examine and better understand the factors behind specific outcomes or experiences. Such a session proceeds as follows:

- *Defining the objectives of the session*: The organizer explains the purpose of the cause-and-effect analysis session. It can aim for a deeper understanding of specific events or results within the teambuilding program.
- *Selection of events or results to be analyzed*: The team determines which events or results will be analyzed within the session. These can be key moments within the teambuilding program, such as specific activities, interactions between team members, etc.
- *Identifying root causes*: Participants are encouraged to identify and discuss the factors or actions that contributed to the selected event or outcome. They should try to go beyond the obvious causes and explore deeper issues.
- *Examining Effects and Impact*: Participants discuss the immediate and long-term effects of the event or outcome under consideration. They should focus on both the positive aspects and those that can be improved.
- *Brainstorming solutions and improvements*: The team shares ideas and suggestions on how the analyzed event or outcome could have been handled better or how certain problems can be avoided in the future.
- *Establish action plans*: Depending on the discussions, the team can establish concrete steps to avoid or better manage similar events in the future. Each member can contribute ideas to improve processes.

- *Responsibilities and follow-up*: Determine who will be responsible for implementing the action plans and how progress will be monitored.
- *Session conclusions and summaries*: The organizer closes the session with a summary of the discussions and actions set. The importance of lessons learned from cause-and-effect analysis can be emphasized.

The importance of this activity: It is essential to create an open and respectful environment in cause-and-effect analysis sessions so that participants feel comfortable sharing their thoughts and suggestions. Organizers can also play an important role in guiding and facilitating discussions to ensure an efficient and constructive process.

Activity 8: Group sessions for future planning

Context: The team gathers to set goals and plans for the future, looking at what worked well and what can be improved.

Rules of conduct: Future planning group sessions in teambuilding are a great way to involve team members in defining goals and strategies for the future. This type of session works like this:

- *Introduction and setting the objectives of the session*: The organizer starts by explaining the purpose of the future planning session. It can aim to define short- and long-term goals, set priorities, and create an action plan.
- *Presentation of relevant information*: The organizer can provide relevant information regarding the context, available resources, and any other elements that could influence the future planning of the team.
- *Generating Ideas and Contributions*: Team members are encouraged to contribute ideas and suggestions regarding goals and directions the team should pursue in the future. These contributions can cover aspects such as professional development, project objectives, improving collaboration, etc.
- *Discussion and prioritization*: Participants discuss the generated ideas and reach a consensus on the key goals the team wants to achieve in the future. Priorities can also be set to ensure that resources and efforts are directed to the most important issues.

- *Defining success indicators*: The team establishes clearly defined success indicators for each goal. These indicators will help to assess progress and monitor the achievement of objectives.
- *Setting deadlines and responsibilities*: Each objective should have a clear deadline and be assigned to a person or group responsible for its implementation.
- *Create a detailed action plan*: The team works together to create a detailed action plan that includes the concrete steps needed to achieve each goal.
- *Summary of the session and setting of the next steps*: The organizer closes the session with a summary of the discussions and actions set. The importance of each member's commitment to the implementation of the action plan can be emphasized.

Activity 9: Learning sessions from previous experiences

Context: Team members share lessons learned from previous projects or activities and discuss how they can apply these learnings in the future.

Rules of conduct: Learning sessions from previous experiences in team-building are an effective way to extract valuable learning from the team's past experiences. The sessions are conducted as follows:

Introduction and goal setting: The organizer starts by explaining the purpose of the learning session from previous experiences. It may aim to identify lessons learned from past experiences and apply them in the future.

Selection of experiences to analyze: The team decides on specific past experiences or events to be analyzed in the session. These can be moments of success, challenges, or any other significant event for the team.

Event Analysis: Participants are encouraged to reflect on selected events and identify key factors that contributed to that outcome. They should try to identify both the positive aspects and those that can be improved.

Identify lessons learned: The team discusses lessons learned from past experiences. These may include both practical aspects and approaches or attitudes that had an impact on the outcome.

Brainstorming for improvements: Participants contribute ideas and suggestions on how past experiences could have been handled better or how certain problems can be avoided in the future.
Establish action plans: Based on the discussions, the team can establish concrete steps to apply the learning in the future. Each member can contribute ideas to improve processes.
Responsibilities and follow-up: Determine who will be responsible for implementing the action plans and how progress will be monitored.
Session conclusions and summaries: The organizer closes the session with a summary of the discussions and actions set. The importance of applying learnings in practice to improve team performance can be emphasized.

Activity 10: Simulations of difficult situations and constructive feedback

Context: Team members participate in simulated scenarios where they have to give and receive feedback in a constructive way, learning to manage critical situations.

Rules of conduct: Simulations of difficult situations and constructive feedback in teambuilding are effective ways to allow team members to practice critical skills in a controlled environment and receive feedback to improve. The sequence of the implementation stages of these simulations is as follows:

- *Preparing the simulation scenario*: The organizer creates a realistic and relevant scenario involving a difficult situation that the team might face in their regular activities.
- *Explaining the objectives*: The organizer shares the objectives of the simulation session and emphasizes the importance of practice and feedback for development.
- *Roles and Responsibilities*: Participants are assigned specific roles within the simulation. Each team member plays a specific role that involves interactions and decisions within the scenario.
- *Simulation run*: The scenario is played realistically. Participants actively engage in interactions and make decisions based on their roles. It

is important to create a safe environment where participants feel comfortable trying their skills.

- *Performance observation and recording*: The organizer or members of the delivery team can observe and record the performance of each participant during the simulation.
- *Constructive feedback session*: After the simulation is over, a constructive feedback session is organized. Participants receive specific and constructive feedback on how they handled the difficult situation, including strengths and suggestions for improvement.
- *Reflecting on learnings*: Participants are encouraged to reflect on the feedback received and identify key learnings that they can apply in real work situations.
- *Replay if necessary (optional)*: If necessary, the simulation can be repeated to give participants another chance to improve their skills.

The importance of this activity: Challenge simulations and constructive feedback can be valuable tools for team development. These activities provide the opportunity to practice practical skills and receive specific guidance to improve. It is essential that feedback is given in a constructive way so that team members feel motivated to develop.

Bibliography

Burke, A. (2011) Group Work: How to Use Groups Effectively, *The Journal of Effective Teaching 11*(2) 87–95.

Ciucurel, M. (2005). *Planificarea Resurselor Manageriale. Antrenarea Competentelor Psihologice si Sociale ale Managerilor in Organizatiile Romanesti*. Craiova: Editura Universitaria,.

Constantinescu, D., & Girboveanu S. R. (2021). *Comunicare Organizationala*. Editia II. Editura Pro Universitaria <PUN978-606-26-1376-1>.

Dumitrache, S. (2016). *Catre Tine … 13 Exercitii De Autocunoastere, Dezvoltare Personala Si Well-Being*, Editura SPER. ISBN <973-742-204 X>.

Koziol, C. (2021) Journaling's Impact on Mental Health. *UWL Journal of Undergraduate Research XXIV*.

Pease, A., & Pease, B. (2020). *Abilitati de Comunicare*, Ed. II. Editura Curtea Veche.

Petrick, J. F. (2004). The Roles of Quality, Value and Satisfaction in Predicting Cruise

Passengers' Behavioral Intentions. *Journal of Travel Research 42*(4), 397–407.

Priest, S. (n.d.). *Experiencia*. <http://www.tarrak.com/EXP/exp.htm>, accessed at 12.12.2012.

Reggio, R., Carducci, B., Nave, C., & Mio, J. (2020). *Social Skills in the Workplace in The Wiley Encyclopedia of Personality and Individual Differences*. <https://doi.org/10.1002/9781119547181.ch352>.

Reinsch, N. L., & Shelby, A. N. (1997). What Communication Abilities Do Practitioners Need? Evidence from MBA Students. *Business Communication Quarterly 60*(4), 7–29. <https://doi.org/10.1177/108056999706000401>.

Reisinger, Y., & Turner, L. W. (2003). *Cross-cultural Behaviour in Tourism: Concepts and Analysis.* Oxford: Butterworth-Heinemann.

Roşu D. (2008), *Tehnici de Animare – Team Building Montan.* Universitaria Craiova

Rosu, D., (2015). Participants Profile in Sport Airsoft, *Procedia—Social and Behavioral Sciences, 180* (p. 1316–21). <https://doi.org/10.1016/j.sbspro.2015.02.270>.

Rosu, D., & Miroiu, M. (2018). Relationship of Physical Education and Sport in a Mountainous Environment Together with Intelligent Specialities. *Journal of Physical Education and Sport 18*, 2116–21. <https://doi.org/10.7752/jpes.2018.s5319>.

Rosu, D., (2019), Multidisciplinary Connotations of the Development of Cycling in the Life of Society. *Education Facing Contemporary World Issues*. <https://doi.org/10.15405/epsbs.2019.08.03.90>

Roşu D., Cojanu F., Ştefănică V. & Enache S. (2022), *Experimental Management of Work Collectives through Social and Socialization Activities 22*, 1742–47. <https://doi.org/10.7752/jpes.2022.07218>.

Rutten, B. P. F., Hammels, C., Geschwind, N., Menne-Lothmann, C., Pishva, E., Schruers, K., van den Hove, D., Kenis, G., van Os J., & Wichers, M. (2013). Resilience in Mental Health: Linking Psychological and Neurobiological Perspectives. *Acta Psychiatrica Scandinavia*. <https://doi.org/10.1111/acps.12095>.

Schley, T., & van Woerkom, M. (2014). Reflection and Reflective Behaviour in Work Teams. In C Harteis, A. Rausch, & J. Seifried (Eds.) Discourses on Professional Learning. *Professional and Practice-based Learning (Vol. 9)*. Springer. <https://doi.org/10.1007/978-94-007-7012-6_7>.

Stoykov, A. (2020). Dynamics of Assertive Behavior in the Social Work. *Amazonia Investiga 9*(28). <http://dx.doi.org/10.34069/AI/2020.28.04.2>.

Williams, P., & Soutar G. N. (2009). Value, Satisfaction and Behavioral Intentions in an Adventure Tourism Context. *Annals of Tourism Research 36*(3), 413–38. <https://doi.org/10.1016/j.annals.2009.02.002>.

CHAPTER 10

Relaxation and socialization activities

Daniel Roşu, Andreea Laura Bădulescu, and Manuela Mihaela Ciucurel

Summary: The relaxation and socializing activities carried out at the end of a teambuilding action are essential for strengthening the bonds between team members. They give participants the opportunity to relax, interact in a less formal setting, and strengthen personal relationships. The characteristics of these activities include a friendly and open atmosphere, stimulating communication, strengthening interpersonal relationships, promoting team spirit, offering relaxing moments, supporting mutual knowledge, creating distinctive memories, promoting the balance between professional and personal life, or opening the way for collaborations future Relaxation and socializing activities are most popular when organizations resort to teambuilding. However, their effects are inferior to educational, development, or reorientation-redirection programs aimed at teambuilding. While some activities may have elements from more than one category, in general, teambuilding combines these elements to create a holistic program that supports team development in multiple aspects, both personal and professional.

Keywords: Fun and non-competitive competitions, outdoor excursions, nature walks, museum visits, informal networking sessions

The relaxation and socializing activities carried out at the end of a teambuilding action are optional. They can be planned to give team members an opportunity to relax, have fun, and interact in a more relaxed and informal environment. In the background, these activities also aim to strengthen interpersonal relationships, and connections between team members, and increase the feeling of cohesion and camaraderie. These activities provide a conducive environment for team members to get to know each other better and collaborate effectively.

10.1. The place of relaxation and socialization programs within the activities of organizations

In Simon Priest's view, the programs used by large corporations are of four types:

- Type 1—recreational activities,
- Type 2—education activities,
- Type 3—development activities, and
- Type 4—reorientation-redirection activities.

Although the author does not make direct references to teambuilding, its dimensions raise a decipherment between the four types of activities mentioned above. There are notable differences between these types of activities, as can be seen in Table 10.1.

Table 10.1. The effects of different types of teambuilding programs

Types of programs	Recreational	Educational	Of development	Of reorientation, redirection
The effects of the programs	It changes the way people feel	It changes the way people feel and think	It changes the way people feel, think, and behave	It changes the way people feel, think, behave, and show resistance to change

How recreational should teambuilding be? The answer to this question brings into question two scenarios:

- Scenario 1—when teambuilding is organized for recreational purposes, including only fun and socializing activities.
- Scenario 2—when teambuilding has educational (Leal-Rodriguez et al., 2014), development (Hsu et al., 2011) or reorientation-redirection objectives and at the end of the activities only a few recreational, fun and/or socializing activities are organized.

From our observations made on 126 such events held in Romania between 2009 and 2023, no less than 69 events (54.8%) had recreational activities as their main objective (scenario 1 above)! This result shows that in the business or corporate environment in Romania, the role of teambuilding is not sufficiently well understood. We make this interpretation precisely to emphasize the fact that it is efficient and rational for recreational activities, including relaxation and socialization, to be organized only as the final part (with optional status) of a teambuilding event.

However, there are scientifically proven situations in companies where the organization of recreational teambuilding, including relaxation and socializing activities, is a priority. There are situations where people in work teams need recreational teambuilding that they particularly appreciate.

Recreational activities, which include relaxation and socializing, are designed to change the way people feel. Within them, participants are encouraged to have fun, re-energize, relax, socialize, learn new things, acquire new skills, etc. They can be considered safe ways of entertainment and are meant to alter the mood of all participants. The objectives of these programs are focused on organizational development (OD), the preparation and realization of the program design, being done without much effort on the part of the facilitators.

Socializing in teambuilding activities provides opportunities for team members to interact outside of the regular work environment. This can help build stronger bonds between colleagues and develop trust and effective communication. In order to socialize advantageously, people need social skills, which are the expression of the high development of the human being, their presence having multiple benefits in psychological, cognitive, and organic terms. Developing social skills is an absolutely necessary process for maintaining psycho-social and physical well-being. Regarding the relationship between social skills and mental health, studies confirm that their optimization can have a significant role in the treatment of schizophrenia (Liberman, 1996), anxiety (Curan, 1975), loneliness (Adams et al., 1988), addictions (Monty, Myers, 1994), depression (Bellack et al., 1987), respectively behaviors with negative social impact (Verduyn et al., 1990).

Relaxation focuses on reducing stress and tension; integrating it into teambuilding events can encourage participants to feel more comfortable and open during activities. A relaxed atmosphere can make social interactions more enjoyable and facilitate collaboration.

Numerous studies have indicated that when people experience positive emotions, they are more open to the world/outside, interested in accumulating new information in order to integrate it with the already known, in order to create new constructions with the role of adaptation, problem solving, and personal optimization. Thus, charismatic people show specific behaviors and attitudes of attraction and social integration, not because they have access to a series of techniques that most would not possess, but because they have integrated high social skills, being aware of the role and multiple their benefits, showing interest in personal development and social optimization. On the other hand, negative affective states facilitate the withdrawal and maladaptive centering of the person exclusively on the self, which can create a downward spiral of emotions through which the interest in the outside world, information, colleagues, or new situations existing in the environment decreases. carry out existence (the socio-professional context). A similar mechanism is found in the case of sadness, which can cause the person to excessively relive past experiences that resulted in failure, which reduces the ability to assimilate new information that could serve them in order to adapt to current situations.

An example of an emotion that can alter the state of relaxation—causing difficulties in socializing—is anxiety, especially in situations that require personal expression: meetings, requests from superiors, colleagues, or activities specific to the job description that put the person in difficulty when they have to interact with others. It thus becomes difficult to initiate or maintain communication when problems related to managing one's own social anxiety state arise. Coping with shyness, anxiety, and insecurity should be understood as an essential goal to reach a desirable personal level, which allows access to a comfortable psycho-physical state, based on relaxation/relaxation, to optimize self-confidence and trust in others.

Essentially, teambuilding provides opportunities for learning and development (activities of types 2 and 3 in Simon Priest's classification) in a non-formal environment, where participants can experience and apply the knowledge gained in a practical and interactive way, thus contributing to their personal and professional growth.

Educational programs are intended to change the way people feel and believe (gaining awareness of needs, understanding, and acquiring new knowledge and concepts, understanding new ways to change old concepts of life or family, etc.). Development programs are designed to change the way people feel, believe, and behave (increase functional, positive behavior by improving interpersonal and intrapersonal relationships). It is thus observed that developmental programs achieve superior effects to educational programs and both are superior to recreational programs that include relaxation and socialization.

Thus, the organization of educational programs, as opposed to recreational ones, considers the following arguments:

- Develops social and communication skills: In teambuilding activities, participants are often encouraged to work together to solve problems, communicate effectively, and improve their teamwork skills. These skills are essential not only in a work environment but also in everyday life.

- Improves interpersonal relationships: Teambuilding provides opportunities for participants to create stronger bonds with each other. While working together to achieve common goals, people get to know each other better and develop mutual trust.
- Encourages leadership and accountability: Teambuilding activities can provide a platform to identify and develop leadership skills among participants (Savelsbergh et al., 2015). By encouraging the assumption of responsibility and decision-making as a team, individual leadership capabilities are developed.
- Involves learning through hands-on experience: Teambuilding often places participants in real or simulated situations that require strategic thinking, decision-making, and creative problem-solving. By tackling these hands-on tasks, participants learn in an interactive and memorable way.
- Promotes collaboration and cohesion: One of the main objectives of teambuilding is to promote collaboration and cohesion in a team. Participants learn to appreciate their colleagues, understand diversity, and develop their working skills in an intercultural environment.

However, teambuilding can also serve as an effective tool in the process of professional reorientation or redirection (type 4 of Simon Priest's classification), intended especially for members of work groups that show resistance to change. They provide participants with valuable opportunities for self-discovery, development, and exploration of new career directions or interests. Reorientation-redirection programs, much more complex than recreational ones (for relaxation and socialization), consider the following arguments:

- Identify skills and interests: During teambuilding activities, the individual skills of the participants as well as their interests can be observed and evaluated. Through varied activities and challenges, previously unexplored talents, abilities, or preferences can be discovered or strengthened.
- Explore and develop new skills: Teambuilding can provide opportunities to learn and develop new skills that are relevant to different fields or professional positions (Zappa & Lomi, 2016). These

activities can be designed to provide participants with experiences that enhance their skills in specific areas, such as leadership, problem-solving, or effective communication.
- Create new career perspectives: Through teambuilding exercises and discussions focused on personal and professional goals, participants can gain a better understanding of their real interests and the direction in which they want to develop their careers. This can help them reassess their goals and redirect their efforts in new directions or career opportunities.
- Builds confidence and ensures support: By participating in teambuilding activities that require collaboration and communication, participants can gain confidence in their abilities and develop closer bonds with colleagues. This can lead to an increased level of comfort in exploring new areas and career possibilities, knowing that they have the support and backing of the team.
- Facilitate transition between roles or fields: Teambuilding can help facilitate the transition from one professional role or field to another, providing participants with a safe and stimulating space to learn and grow in a way that supports professional change.

The most effective way of applying reorientation-redirection programs is to resort to adventure-type activities or through extreme sports (see Chapter 1). However, this is done by following some basic recommendations, among which we mention:

- The first recommended step is to assess participants to understand their fitness level, abilities, and personal limits. It is essential to ensure that the proposed activities are appropriate for the abilities and comfort levels of each participant.
- Adventure activities or extreme sports require planning and preparation. In this sense, the facilitators will necessarily call on qualified professionals or specialized teams to provide appropriate training and supervision during the activities.
- Safety is of crucial importance. All safety measures are considered and respected during the activities. Protective equipment and safety instructions must be available and followed by all participants.

- Adventure activities and extreme sports can help participants push their personal limits and develop confidence in their own abilities. Facilitators will encourage calculated risk-taking but emphasize the importance of assessing and managing it responsibly.

In conclusion, teambuilding is usually associated with recreational activities that include fun and socializing. But as we have shown above, teambuilding activities can be classified into several categories (recreational, educational, development, and redirection) depending on their objectives and the way they contribute to the personal and professional growth of the participants. While some activities may have elements from more than one category, in general, teambuilding combines these elements to create a holistic program that supports team development in multiple aspects, both personal and professional. The specific objectives of each activity may vary depending on the needs and goals of the group involved.

10.2. Personality and temperament—influencing factors in the development of social skills

The individual's ability to socialize is related to personality traits and temperament. By "personality" is meant the stable element of a person's behavior or what characterizes and differentiates them from other people. Personality combines both general traits and particular traits, is formed from birth and continues to develop throughout life, based on heredity but strongly influenced by the external environment.

The composition of the personality includes temperament, intelligence, character, and creativity. At the same time, personality refers to the characteristic patterns of a human being, in terms of the way of thinking, feeling, or acting (behaviors and attitudes).

Of all the components of personality, temperament is the innate dimension, so having solid information about temperamental characteristics would participate in identify the best strategies for training and developing social skills. If all the other components of the personality can be "educated" under social influence, temperament is a "given" with a significant role in what presupposes the ability to relax and social ability, the specific temperament not being influenced by the action of external factors.

Temperament is an innate emotional disposition based on neural and hormonal mechanisms (Thomas et al., 1970). Temperament is written in the genetic code and determines the temperamental structure of the personality, that is, temperament energetically supports all psychic processes (their intensity, flexibility, and balance).

Temperament types are equipotent, that is, none is better or less good than another, each temperament type having specific advantages and disadvantages. Often, temperamental types are found at the human level in the combined version, in which the features of a certain type become more accentuated or predominant. Very rarely will one meet a person dominated by a single, pure temperamental type. Temperament is not neutral from an adaptive point of view but represents an interface between the person and the world, acting as a mediator between the intensity, duration, and significance of external influences and effects in the psycho-behavioral sphere (e.g., the role of temperamental traits in determining interpersonal relationships).

Having information about one's own personality structure and temperamental characteristics becomes a necessity in relation to optimizing social skills, which have been shown to be very important in determining and sustaining health on all levels throughout life.

10.3. Types of relaxation and socializing activities

The most obvious characterization of relaxation and socializing activities refers to the fact that they are *events in the form of action* and, as we have already shown, they are most often used when organizations aim to organize teambuilding. Among the common ways of relaxing and socializing, we can mention:

- Social Events: These may include parties, gala dinners, team games, or other social events that provide an opportunity for team members to socialize in a more informal setting.
- Fun games and contests: These activities involve team members participating in fun, non-competitive games and contests that create a relaxed atmosphere and facilitate interaction.

- Excursions or nature walks: These may include outdoor excursions, nature walks, or other activities in the surrounding environment that provide a break from the regular work environment and allow members to relax and enjoy time together.
- Cultural or artistic activities: These involve attending cultural events, visiting museums, art galleries, or other cultural venues that provide a relaxing and educational experience.
- Yoga or meditation sessions: These activities are designed to help team members relax, focus, and release stress through a physical and mental relaxation practice.
- Cooking or wine tasting workshops: These activities involve taking part in cooking sessions or wine tastings, providing an opportunity to work together in a relaxed and fun way.
- Informal networking sessions: These provide the opportunity for team members to socialize and get to know each other better in a less formal environment, favouring the building of personal relationships.

These activities are essential to create a pleasant work environment and strengthen relationships between team members (Roşu *et al.* 2022). They help foster a team culture where members feel comfortable interacting and enjoying the presence of their colleagues. It is important that these activities suit the interests and preferences of the team and that the organizers ensure a pleasant and relaxing environment for all participants.

10.4. Examples of relaxation and socializing activities

The activities below can provide conclusive examples of each of the types of activities intended to complete teambuilding as follows:

Activities like social events

Description: Activities that match the atmosphere and objectives of the teambuilding event, considering the preferences and needs of the participants. It is important to create a relaxing and joyful environment so that all participants leave with fond memories and a sense of achievement and team connection.

Rules of conduct: Among the concrete ways of holding some social events, we can mention:

Awards and recognition evening: An awards ceremony is organized for participants who have distinguished themselves in various activities or made significant contributions to the success of the event. Diplomas, trophies, or small symbolic gifts can be given on this occasion.

- *Festive dinner:* A dinner is organized in a pleasant setting, where participants can socialize and relax after a day full of activities.
- *Relaxing games and competitions:* Fun games and light competitions are organized to involve all participants. These can be both board games and outdoor activities. A suitable application of relaxation and compulsion games could be achieved by using the kin-ball game (see Figure 10.1).
- *Disco or theme party:* If space and atmosphere allow, parties can be organized with music, dance, and a specific theme to bring more fun.
- *Networking sessions:* An atmosphere conducive to socialization and interaction between participants is created. It can be informal discussions, exchange of ideas, or even short individual presentations.
- *Reflection and feedback sessions:* Whenever the aim is to encourage open communication and get feedback from the participants, it is recommended to organize sessions where everyone can share their opinion about the event and where everyone can propose improvements for the future.
- *Voluntary activities or social responsibility:* Involvement of participants in a charitable or voluntary activity is beneficial to give a deeper meaning to the event and to strengthen the team spirit (Rosu & Miroiu, 2018).
- *Presentation of slideshows or video collages:* Invite participants to share moments and memories during the event in the form of photo slideshows or video collages.
- *Relaxation and mindfulness sessions:* Organizing yoga, meditation, or other activities to help participants relax and connect on a deeper level.
- *Outdoor recreational activities:* If the event took place in a natural environment, walks, trips, or other outdoor activities can be organized to provide an opportunity to explore the surroundings.
- *Closing Gala:* An elegant gala is organized to mark the end of the event, with great food, live music, and thank you speeches.

Figure 10.1. Kin ball—relaxing games.

10.4.1. Activities like: funny games and contests

General description: Games with fun themes that match the atmosphere and preferences of the group at the end of the event.

General rules of conduct: The comfort level of the participants will be considered and the facilitators will ensure that everyone feels included and has fun. Although the examples can be numerous, we will still offer some ideas:

Activity 1: Human egg relay

Participants form teams and must carry an egg on a spoon to the finish line without dropping the egg.

Activity 2: Dance of the statues

Any cheerful song can be chosen. When the music stops, all participants must remain in statue position. The last person to move is eliminated. An example of the application can be seen in Figure 10.2.

Figure 10.2. Dance of the statues.

Activity 3: Throwing socks

In a team game, participants try to throw pairs of socks into a basket at a distance.

Activity 4: Defense balloon

Participants are divided into teams and must protect a water balloon from bursting while trying to pop the other teams' balloons.

Activity 5: Running with the sack

Participants compete in a sack race, with their feet in the sacks, to the finish line.

Activity 6: Guess the song

A song guessing game is organized where sounds or pieces of music are played, and participants try to identify the song.

Activity 7: Funny sketches

Groups can create and perform short comedy sketches that showcase their improvisational and humorous skills.

Activity 8: Dance competition

A dance competition is organized in which each team presents a previously prepared choreography. An example of the application can be seen in Figure 10.3.

Figure 10.3. Dance competition.

Activity 9: Fun quiz

A set of fun and funny questions is created, possibly related to the experiences during the teambuilding.

Activity 10: Race of unusual objects

Participants must carry an unusual object from one end of the playing field to the other (e.g., a lemon or a wooden spoon).

Activity 11: Dance of the statues with the team

Participants have to dance to the music, but when the music stops, they have to lock in a specific position according to a given theme.

Activity 12: The "Volleyball with a blanket" game

On a field where a volleyball net is arranged, the collective is divided into two teams, as in a classic volleyball match. Each team will use a blanket

Figure 10.4. The "Clock Game."

to handle the ball that will be thrown into the other court only through a collective team effort. The ball must not be touched by any participant. When the ball is not caught in the blanket and falls to the ground, that team loses a point, play being restarted by the other team by throwing the ball through the blanket. Materials needed: net, two squares, volleyball, marked court.

Activity 13: The "Clock Game"

Participants are seated in a circle holding hands. Some sheets are placed in a circle with the numbers 12, 3, 6, 9 representing the hours and thus forming a "clock." At the signal of the animator, who says one hour (for Example 6), the circle must rotate half a turn so that the player who was originally at 12 o'clock ends up next to the number 6. The animator can say, for example, "it's been 12 hours," and the circle must make a complete rotation. The goal of the game is for the participants to communicate so that they stop at the set times without letting go of their hands.

Materials needed: 4 A4 sheets.

Activity variants: The game can be played outdoors and indoors. A variation of the game is for the participants to sit on the floor when they arrive at the appointed time. Another variation is to time the rotations when forming two "clocks."

Activity 14: The "Magic Word" game

Description: The group of participants is divided into two teams, seated face to face, bent forward, with the trunk bent at 90 degrees. Between the two rows, a row of objects (scoops, bottles, hats, gloves, etc.) is placed, each pair having an object, located at an equal distance of about 30–50 cm from the players. *Rules of conduct*: at the animator's command, the pair will simultaneously perform arm movements. Thus, at the command knee/back/nose/neck/eyes/ears/etc., the participants will touch these parts of their own body. Between these commands will be interspersed the command that will include the magic word that will represent the object between the players (scoop, bottle, hat, gloves). At this command, the fastest player will grab the designated object. The team that takes the object in the middle the most times wins. An example of the application can be seen in Figure 10.5.

Figure 10.5. The “magic word” game.

Activity 15: The “X and 0” game

Description: The game is played in the form of a relay. The group is divided into two teams behind a starting line. In front of the starting line, at a variable distance of 5–20 m, a square with a side of 3 m is drawn on the ground, in which nine quadrants with a side of 1 m are delimited. Each team will benefit from three similar objects (hoes, t-shirts, hats, scarves) of the same type and color.

Rules of conduct: at the moment of the start, one member of each team moves quickly to the square, where he will place the object in one of the inner quadrants, quickly returning to the starting place, touching the next colleague, who will try to place the second object in one of the quadrants. The placement of the third object will aim to form a line, a column, or a diagonal with the two previously placed objects. Objects cannot be placed in a square occupied by objects of one's own team or of the opposing team. If the three objects have been placed in the squares without achieving game closure, the player, in turn, will have to move one of his own objects to another free square in order to close the game. An example of the application can be seen in Figure 10.6.

Figure 10.6. The "X and 0" game.

Materials needed: Adhesive tapes or strings to delimit the quadrants, three similar objects for each team.

Activity 16: The "Ninja" game

Description: All participants are seated in a circle with a distance of about 1–1.5 m between them. At the start command "Ninja!," all players playfully assume a fun battle stance. One of the players is designated to start the game by making a quick flick of the palm of the hand or the back of the palm of any player near him. The player being attacked is allowed to make one defensive move, after which he will remain stationary in the resulting position. The next clockwise player will have to make an attack move to a nearby player, and the attacked player will make a defense move.

Rules of conduct: All attacking moves will be considered successful when the palm or back of any player's palm is touched. Players will remain stationary until it is their turn to attack or when they are forced to defend. Whenever a subject is touched on the palm or the back of it, it will exit the game. The game will continue until the most agile player remains untouched on the palms.

An example of the application can be seen in Figure 10.7.

Figure 10.7. The "Ninja" game.

Activity 17. The "Crabs and Shrimps" game

Description: The players are divided into two teams, facing each other, at a distance of 1 m from the line that separates them. At the command of the animator, the team that is called must catch players from the other team, who, in order to save themselves, must reach a safe space, arranged at a variable distance.

Rules of conduct: Players who are touched are taken prisoner on the opposing team.

Activity variants: The starting positions can be different: from crouching with the back/facing the opponent, from lying on the back/facing with the head/feet facing the opponent, etc.

Activity 18: The "Gestures" game

Description: Through this game, the participants try to remember in order the gestures made by their teammates.

Rules of conduct: The participants are divided into groups of a maximum seven players, they are seated in a circle, performing one gesture in turn clockwise. Each player will have to imitate the previous gestures performed by teammates in order and add their own gesture. As the game progresses, the suite of gestures performed by each participant will be larger and larger.

Materials needed: No materials needed.

Activity variants: The game can be played outdoors and indoors.

Activity 19: Game "Change direction!"

Description: The participants are arranged in a semicircle, sitting on their knees with support on their palms, shoulder to shoulder. At the animator's command, the left hand of each participant moves between the arms of the player on his left.

Rules of conduct: One of the participants hits the ground with the right palm and the game starts. The player to his right imitates the palming motion, which will be repeated by all players in turn until a player randomly decides to perform two quick taps on the ground with his right palm, after which he also performs a single tap into the ground with the left palm, changing the direction of action of the whole group. Next, the player on the left side executes a single stroke with the left hand, a movement that will be repeated successively by all the players on the left side until the moment when a player performs two strokes on the ground with the left hand, changing the direction again. The player who makes a mistake is eliminated.

Materials needed: There is no need.

Variants: At the first mistake, players are penalized with the disposition of the hand that performed the improper backhand. On the second mistake, he is eliminated.

Activity 20: The game "Guess the character"

Description: The participants have to guess, based on the explanations of their colleagues, the name of the character written on a post-it and stuck on each one's back.

Rules of conduct: Participants move around and can ask each participant one random question about their character's characteristics written on the back; they can receive one question about the character in front of them, then they will move to another participant for a new piece of information.

Materials needed: Post-it.

Activity variants: The game can be played outdoors and indoors.

Activity 21: The "Lava lake crossing" game

Context: The Lava lake crossing game in teambuilding activities is a fun and interactive exercise that also provides learning opportunities for the team by testing collaboration, communication, and strategy skills. It involves simulating a dangerous space (lava) that the team must cross using a limited set of "points" (objectives) without falling into the "lava" (dangerous space).

Rules of conduct: It is explained to the participants that the space around them represents the "lava lake" and that they must cross it to reach their destination, using the available hints. Participants are divided into equal teams and shown the destination to which they must reach. This can be a point on the floor, a marked area, or a predetermined objective.

The team must reach the destination without falling into the "lava lake." This means they only have to use the hints to cross the dangerous space. Participants must stay on the cues while using them. If they touch the "lava" (the space between the hints), they are "eliminated" from the game. The team will devise a strategy to use the clues effectively and reach the destination with as many members as possible left.

Participants must find ways to place the clues (targets) in the "lava lake" to reach the destination. They can communicate and collaborate to find the best crossing strategy, moving and rearranging cues to reach their destination safely.

Materials needed: The play space (a hall, outdoor area, or large space to carry out the activity) and tiles, logs, paper, colored tape, or other objects (bridges) to cross the "lava lake."

Importance of this activity: The team must collaborate and communicate effectively to find the best solutions for crossing the "lava lake." It is important to develop an effective strategy to use the available hints intelligently and reach your destination safely.

Activity 22. The "Pyramids"

Context: The "Pyramids" is a fun game that involves establishing a proper strategy, team coordination, and communication between group members.

Rules of conduct: This game should take place in a large open space (corridor, meeting room, cafe, etc.). The team divides into groups of four to six people, and each team receives 10 paper cups. They are asked to form a line, leaving a space of 2–3 m between each person. This is the start of the race against the clock.

The first person in each row must create a pyramid with four cups at the base. After he finishes, the second player must help him carry the pyramid to the first set stage (on the ground or on a table). Players can slide it across the floor or carry it, but if the pyramid collapses, they will have to rebuild it immediately before continuing their journey. Once the pyramid is in place, the second player knocks it down and rebuilds it before the next player helps transport it to the next stage. The cycle continues until the pyramid reaches its destination. The team that reaches the destination first wins.

Advantages of this activity: It is a fun game, ideal for taking a break during the day, and learning better communication and teamwork.

Activity 23. Wall of memories

Rules of conduct: A whiteboard and sticky notes must be purchased for this game. On the board, make a list of different work themes (e.g., first day at work, team party, business trip, etc.). Several sticky notes are distributed to each classmate, and each is asked to write down their favorite memories or accomplishments related to one or more of these themes. Everyone is invited to share them with the team for old times' sake, and notes are taped to the board as the stories unfold.

Advantages of this activity: The game is a fun way to end the week, day, or workshop by sharing positive experiences with colleagues. At the end of a business trip or multi-day workshop, the lighter version can be used by asking everyone to share their favorite memory or greatest achievement from the past few days.

Activity 24: Excursions and nature walks

Context: Walking activities, safe and accessible for all participants. Consideration will be given to the fitness level of the group and the provision of additional equipment or guidance where necessary. An example of the application can be seen in Figure 10.8.

Figure 10.8. Excursions and nature walks.

Rules and instructions for conduct: Among the ideas common to the performance of these activities, we mention:

- *Hike or guided walk:* Choose an attractive destination for a nature walk, such as a forest, national park, or mountain area. Facilitators will ensure they have a guide or mentor to provide interesting information about the environment.
- *Visit to a historical or cultural site:* An excursion is organized to a historical or cultural site in the area, where participants can learn new things and explore fascinating places (Stefanica & Rosu, 2018).
- *Bike ride:* If there is access to bikes, organize an outdoor ride, which can be a fun and active way to explore the surroundings (Rosu, 2019). The facilitators will ensure that the level of knowledge of the participants in the matter of riding a bicycle is appropriate, and that the number of these equipments is consistent with the number and particularities of the development of the participants.
- *Themed trail hike:* Choose a trail with a specific theme, such as bird watching, plant recognition, or geological exploration. Facilitators will prepare informative materials to make the experience educational and fun.
- *Picnic and relaxation:* Choose a suitable place in nature to organize a picnic. Facilitators will make sure there is delicious food and drinks, as well as comfortable blankets or chairs.
- *Boating or yachting:* If there is access to the water, a suitable boat ride can be organized that can carry the group of participants and that can provide a memorable and fun experience.
- *Nature photography course:* With the help of a professional or amateur photographer, a walk in nature can be guided to offer tips for capturing the most beautiful images.

Activity 25: Cultural or artistic manifestation

Context: Cultural or artistic activities that match the interests and preferences of the group.

Rules and instructions for conduct: These types of activities can help develop creativity and team spirit while providing an opportunity to relax and have fun. Among the suitable ways we can mention:

- *Art or creative workshops:* A workshop is organized where participants can explore various art forms such as painting, sculpture, ceramics, or collage.

- *Cooking class or culinary tasting:* A professional chef is invited to teach participants culinary techniques or organize a tasting of local or international dishes.
- *Theater performance or improvisation:* A theater performance is organized where participants can perform pre-prepared scenarios or create improvisational scenes.
- *Dance workshop or dance lesson:* A dance instructor is invited to teach a specific dance or organize a free dance workshop, where everyone can participate.
- *Music class or singing session:* A musician or music teacher is invited to give basic singing lessons or organize a group singing session. An example of the application can be seen in Figure 10.9.
- *Trip to a museum or art gallery:* A visit to a local museum or art gallery is organized, where participants can admire works of art and learn about the history and culture of the place.

Figure 10.9. Music class or singing session.

- *Traditional or folkloric dance course:* Through an instructor specialized in the traditional dances of the respective region or country, the basic steps are learned, and a small performance can be organized.
- *Language lesson:* An instructor or professor can teach some basic words and phrases in a foreign language, especially if the event took place in a country or region with a different language.
- *Talent competition:* Participants are invited to show their talents, be it singing, dancing, reciting poems, or presenting artistic numbers.
- *Storytelling or creative writing workshop:* A specialist can guide participants in creating stories or creative writing.

Activity 26: Yoga or meditation session

Context: Yoga and meditation sessions can provide a great way to promote relaxation and inner connection, contributing to a calm and deeply comforting end to the event. A qualified and experienced instructor guides participants through a specific session.

Rules and instructions for conduct: Facilitators will ensure that the space is adequate to allow participants to feel comfortable and relaxed. These sessions can have different characters and objectives such as:

- Outdoor yoga session.
- Guided meditation: Based on relaxation and deep self-connection.
- Yoga for balance and inner harmony: it uses specific positions and techniques.
- Energy Restoration Yoga: It focuses on revitalization and recovery, helping participants feel refreshed and energized.
- Yoga for flexibility and mobility: Techniques and positions to support flexibility and mobility of the body.
- Breathing and relaxation session: Correct breathing techniques and tension release are taught.
- Yoga for stress relief and deep relaxation.
- Yoga for focus and mental clarity.
- Meditation in motion (e.g., yoga Nidra): Combining elements of yoga with states of deep relaxation.

- Yoga for emotional and mental balance: Balancing emotions with thinking.

Activity 27: Cooking Workshops or Wine Tasting

Context: Cooking workshops and wine tasting can provide a memorable and fun dining experience for participants.

Rules and instructions for conduct: Facilitators will ensure that qualified and experienced professionals guide these sessions and that appropriate products and equipment are available.

Among the suitable cooking workshops, we can mention:

- Local cooking workshop: Based on the preparation of traditional or local dishes.
- Dessert making workshop: Where you learn how to make delicious desserts such as cakes, tarts, or eclairs.
- Cocktail making session.
- Sushi workshop: Introduction to Japanese cuisine.
- Bread or pastry preparation workshop.
- Healthy cooking class: A nutritionist or healthy chef can offer healthy cooking tips and techniques.

In the case of wine tastings, the sessions may have the following specificities:

- Wine tasting with a sommelier: By inviting a professional sommelier, participants are guided in tasting different types of wine, providing information on varieties, aromas, and pairings.
- Tasting of local wines.
- Wine and chocolate tasting: Combining wines with chocolate offers participants a delicious and sophisticated culinary experience.
- Wine-tasting pairing session: Pairing different types of wines with aperitifs or specific dishes, to offer participants a complex culinary experience.
- Wine selection and serving course: An expert is invited to give advice and instructions on the correct selection, opening, and serving of wines.
- Tasting of rare or fine wines: If possible, participants may be offered the opportunity to taste rare, fine, or collectible wines.

Activity 28: Informal networking

Rules and instructions for conduct: Facilitators will ensure the atmosphere is friendly, open, and relaxed to encourage participants to interact naturally and make genuine connections. Among the typical sessions of this type of activity, we can mention:

- *Conversation cafe:* A cafe-style area is organized where participants can sit in small groups and freely discuss various topics.
- *Speed networking sessions:* Set up a series of quick chat exchanges where participants can exchange contact information.
- *Thematic discussion sessions:* Discussion groups are organized, focused on specific topics related to the industry or common interests.
- *Informal brainstorming sessions:* Relaxed environments are created where participants can share ideas, solutions, and innovative approaches to common challenges.
- *Lounge-style social event:* Set up a cozy space with soft music and seating areas where attendees can connect in an informal way.
- *Share sessions and success stories:* Participants are invited to share stories from their careers, challenges they have overcome, and lessons learned.
- *Open question and answer sessions:* A specialist or speaker is invited for a question-and-answer session where participants can ask their questions and receive advice.

Bibliography

Adler, A. (1996). *Cunoasterea Omului.* Bucuresti: Ed. IRI .

Breil, S. M., Mielke, I., Ahrens, H., Geldmacher T., Sensmeier J., Marschall, B., & Back, Mitja D.. (2022). Predicting Actual Social Skill Expression from Personality and Skill Self-Concepts. *Journal of Intelligence 10*, 48.

Buck, R. (1991). *Temperament, Social Skills, and the Communication of Emotion.* In D. G. Gilbert, J. J. Connolly (Eds.) Personality, Social Skills, and Psychopathology. Perspectives on Individual Differences. Boston, MA: Springer. <https://doi.org/10.1007/978-1-4899-0635-9_4>.

Cioabă, Bogdan (2021). *Flexibilitatea Spațiului Scenic* în *Funcție de Conceptul Regizoral.* Universitaria Craiova.

Ellis, A., Gordon, J. (2020). *Terapia Stresului*. Bucuresti: Trei.

Fexeus, H. (2018). *Manualul Abilitatilor Sociale Superioare*. Bucuresti: Trei.

Gavreliuc, A. (2019). *Psihologia Sociala si Dinamica Personalitatii*. Iasi: Polirom.

Golu, M. (2000). *Fundamentele Psihologiei*. Bucuresti: Ed. Fundaţiei România de Mâine .

Hsu, J., Chang, J., Klein, G., & Jiang, J. (2011). Exploring the Impact of Team Mental Models on Information Utilization and Project Performance in System Development. *International Journal of Project Management 29*(1) 1–12. <http://dx.doi.org/10.1016/j.ijproman.2009.12.001>.

Leal-Rodriguez, A., Roldán, J., Ariza-Montes, J., & Leal-Millán, A. (2014). From Potential Absorptive Capacity to Innovation Outcomes in Project Teams: The Conditional Mediating Role of the Realized Absorptive Capacity in a Relational Learning Context. *International Journal of Project Management 32*, 894–907. <https://doi.org/10.1016/j.ijproman.2014.01.005>.

Lelord, F., & André, C. (2003) *Cum să ne purtăm cu personalităţile dificile*. Bucuresti: Ed. Trei.

Maslow, A. (2008). *Motivatie si personalitate*. Bucuresti: Ed. Trei.

Priest, S. (n.d.). *Experiencia*. <http://www.tarrak.com/EXP/exp.htm>, accesat la 12.12.2012.

Roco, M., (2001). *Creativitate şi inteligenţă emoţională*.Iaşi: Ed. Polirom.

Roşu D. (2008). *Tehnici de animare—team building montan*. Universitaria Craiova.

Rosu, D., (2015). Participants Profile in Sport Airsoft. *Procedia—Social and Behavioral Sciences 180* (1316–21). <https://doi.org/10.1016/j.sbspro.2015.02.270>.

Rosu, D., (2019), Multidisciplinary Connotations of the Development of Cycling in the Life of Society, *Education Facing Contemporary World Issues*. <https://doi.org/10.15405/epsbs.2019.08.03.90>.

Rosu, D., & Miroiu, M. (2018). Relationship of Physical Education and Sport in a Mountainous Environment Together with Intelligent Specialities. *Journal of Physical Education and Sport 18*, 2116–21. <https://doi.org/10.7752/jpes.2018.s5319>.

Roşu, D., Cojanu, F., Ştefănică, V. & Enache, S. (2022). *Experimental Management of Work Collectives through Social and Socialization Activities 22*, 1742–47. <https://doi.org/10.7752/jpes.2022.07218>.

Savelsbergh, C., Poell, R., & van der Heijden, B. (2015). Does Team Stability Mediate the Relationship between Leadership and Team Learning? An Empirical Study among Dutch Project Teams. *International Journal of Project Management 33*, 406–18. <https://doi.org/10.1016/j.ijproman.2014.08.008>.

Stefanica, V., & Rosu, D. (2018). Evaluation of the Working Groups in the Group Cohesion Perspective, in the Project Boboc Camp, 2018. *Journal of Physical Education and Sport 18*, 2134–8. <https://doi.org/10.7752/jpes.2018.s5319>.

Zappa, P., & Lomi, A., (2016). *Knowledge Sharing in Organizations: A Multilevel Network Analysis for the Social Sciences*.London: Springer. <http://dx.doi.org/10.1007/978-3-319-24520-1_14>.

www.ingramcontent.com/pod-product-compliance
Ingram Content Group UK Ltd.
Pitfield, Milton Keynes, MK11 3LW, UK
UKHW021014120926
8556IPUK00040B/1128

9 783631 91583